Three Minutes a Day

VOLUME 40

Other Christopher Books in Print

Better to Light One Candle

and other volumes in the

Three Minutes a Day

series

God Delights in You

THREE MINUTES A DAY
VOLUME 40

Dennis Heaney
President, The Christophers

Stephanie Raha
Editor-in-Chief

Margaret O'Connell
Senior Research Editor

Staff Contributing Editors
Umberto Mignardi
Nicholas Monteleone
Anna Marie Tripodi

Contributors
Joan Bromfield
Monica Ann Yehle-Glick
Karen Hazel Radenbaugh

Contributing Interns
Dunja Dunda
Grace Itiola
Anthony Messina

The Christophers
12 East 48th Street
New York, NY 10017

You are the light of the world. A city built on a hill cannot be hid. No one after lighting a lamp puts it under the bushel basket, but on the lampstand, and it gives light to all in the house. In the same way, let your light shine before others, so that they may see your good works and give glory to your Father in heaven.

MATTHEW 5:14–16

Introduction

This volume of Three Minutes a Day is dedicated to the memory of John Bruno of Staten Island, New York, who died in 2003 at 95. Mr. Bruno was a friend of The Christophers for decades, and thanks to Monsignor Peter Finn, a member of our Board, and Leslie Palma, of the *Staten Island Advance* newspaper, I recently learned more about Mr. Bruno's life of deep spirituality and quiet compassion.

This limited space does not allow for all the details of John Bruno's life, but among the highlights is that he and his wife, Josephine, were married for 72 years. He served one parish for 80 years, beginning as an altar boy, and as an adult attended daily Mass, served as a trustee and, among his gifts, established funding for a media center. Most afternoons, after leaving work at the *Advance,* where he was composing room foreman for nearly 50 years, Mr. Bruno visited the sick in nursing homes and hospitals as well as the homebound–and he did not know many of those he visited.

As his pastor said, "He really lived the way he believed. He was always for the benefit of another person. This is what we sorely need in our society today."

We make this dedication to John Bruno for a life of making a difference and for exemplifying what it means to be a "Christopher."

Dennis Heaney
President, The Christophers

Resolved: To Live with All My Might

At the beginning of the year, many of us make resolutions to develop some worthwhile habit. Have you ever considered making resolutions for the spirit?

Jonathan Edwards, the famed eighteenth century New England theologian and preacher, had some decided opinions on the subject. Here are some of them:

- "Resolved, to live all with my might while I do live.
- "Resolved, never to do anything I should despise or think meanly of in another.
- "Resolved, never to do anything out of revenge.
- "Resolved, never to do anything which I should be afraid to do if it were the last hour of my life."

Everyday we make choices about who and what we are. Our attitudes and our decisions shape our lives. Perhaps we need to pay more attention to the aims of our hearts and the desires of our souls. Let's commit ourselves to our own spiritual resolutions.

Let Your good spirit lead me on a level path. For Your name's sake, O Lord, preserve my life. (Psalm 143:10-11)

Guide me, Spirit of Counsel, in my choices for the good of my whole self and the good of those around me.

Healing Together

When a family faces a crisis, their response can affect more people than they might have imagined.

When Denise Reil's son Scott developed seizures and autism, she turned to prayer. "By praying for Scott, he wasn't necessarily being healed, but we, as a family were being healed," she says. "The walls of self-sufficiency began to crumble and I started to open my heart and home to others."

In time, Reil and supporters established Visitation Home in Yardville, New Jersey. The shared-living residence welcomes persons with developmental disabilities who live as a family with assistants as well as volunteer help.

One father of a developmentally disabled child said, "Up until now, every time I thought about my son's future, it was always with worry. For the first time, I can think about it with hope."

We never know what path God has in mind for us. But we always know He will never let us walk it alone.

Even though I walk through the darkest valley, I fear no evil; for You are with me. (Psalm 23:4)

Guide me and my loved ones, Dear God, in going where You would have us go and doing what You would have us do.

Laughter, the Best Medicine—Really!

There's an old saying about laughter being the best medicine. Now it's been proven medically.

A study by researchers at the University of Maryland found that volunteers who watched a funny movie had blood flow that increased about 22 percent—roughly the same increase as an aerobic workout. Volunteers who watched a violent war movie, however, were found to have a blood flow that actually decreased by 35 percent.

Scientists conjecture that laughter causes the blood vessels to relax, allowing for greater blood flow. A good laugh may also help reduce mental stress.

So go ahead, laugh it up—for your health!

A joyful heart is life itself, and rejoicing lengthens one's life span. (Sirach 30:22)

Lord, help me to find all the humor that life offers—and to share it with others, as well.

A Recipe for Joy

Whether you know her for her hauntingly clear voice, her memorable songs or her ostentatious style, celebrated country-western artist Dolly Parton is hard to forget.

Yet underneath all of the fame, fortune and fripperies of her appearance, there lies a gentle but direct, down-to-earth human being seemingly untouched by the trappings of her career.

In an article in *Guideposts*, Parton listed the five reasons she loves her life. Not one of them included her career or wealth. Instead, she cited friends and family, her love of singing, laughter and a good sense of humor, prayer and the connection she shares with fellow music lovers.

She says simply, "I am a happy person. That is my greatest blessing. Happiness can be yours, too." Happiness is within reach for those who choose it. One's attitude determines the quality of one's life.

A cheerful heart is a good medicine. (Proverbs 17:22)

Help me maintain a positive attitude, Jesus.

Life Valley?

The name "Death Valley" has long been synonymous with acres of barren wasteland. After all, the infamous California desert usually gets only two inches of rain a year. Usually – but not always.

In the opening months of 2005, over six inches of rain fell in the Valley's 3.3 million acres. The deluge led to a sudden bloom of dozens of species of wildflowers, painting the usually desolate valley with vivid colors.

"The flowers are getting better by the day," Death Valley National Park naturalist Charlie Callagan said at the time. "I'm telling folks, 'You may not see it this good again in your lifetime'."

Life can thrive under nearly any conditions. So, too, can hope, if you let it.

Hope that is seen is not hope. For who hopes for what is seen? But if we hope for what we do not see, we wait for it with patience. (Romans 8:24-25)

Lord, help me remember that there is always hope.

Upon This Rock, a Life's Passion

On the surface, some might characterize fourth-generation attorney Charles Welles IV as a "typical" establishment lawyer, particularly given his degrees from both Yale and Harvard Universities.

But there is more to the story and to Welles than the obvious. Welles is also a gifted sculptor who works primarily in marble. He admits his passion is not an easy one to pursue. Marble is expensive; a challenge to ship and maneuver; and difficult to work. Carving marble is also physically demanding and time consuming. One project, for example, took roughly 500 hours to complete.

The challenges pale, however, compared to the joy of sculpting. Welles says sculpting is spiritual in nature, adding, "The spirit is in the creativity."

What are you passionate about? What invigorates you outside of your daily work or role in life. Explore your own new ventures.

I have filled him with divine spirit, with ability, intelligence, and knowledge...to devise artistic designs, to work in gold, silver, and bronze, in cutting stones...in carving wood.
(Exodus 31:3,4)

Holy Spirit, inspire us with a genuine passion for learning and living.

Achieving Your Resolutions

The New Year is a traditional time for people to set goals for themselves. Whether it's giving up a bad habit, losing weight or saving money, too often within weeks or even days, the effort has been abandoned.

The periodical *Bits & Pieces* offers some ideas for success:

- Break up big goals before they break you. Make smaller, attainable objectives and it'll be only a matter of time before your goal is in sight.

- Support yourself. Surround yourself with people who will encourage you to do your best.

- Persevere to get results. Don't give up just because you tried and failed. Figure out what went wrong, make adjustments and try again.

- Be patient with the process. Good habits take years to develop and maintain; bad ones, time to unlearn.

Never give up on yourself or what you want to accomplish.

Run with perseverance the race that is set before us. (Hebrews 12:1)

Heavenly Father, help me to understand what changes I need to make in my life to be the person You want me to be.

Symphony of Life

William Henry Channing, a respected 19th-century clergyman famous for his preaching, wrote a short inspirational piece that is still appreciated and quoted today. Here it is:

"To live content with small means; to seek elegance rather than luxury, and refinement rather than fashion; to be worthy, not respectable, and wealthy, not rich; to study hard, think quietly, talk gently, act frankly; to listen to stars and birds, to babes and sages, with open heart; to bear all cheerfully, do all bravely, await occasions, hurry never.

"In a word, to let the spiritual, unbidden and unconscious, grow up through the common. This is my symphony."

That would be a great deal for anyone to strive for, but it's worthwhile nonetheless. Try asking yourself, "What is my symphony?" The answer will tell you much about yourself.

I will instruct you and teach you the way you should go; I will counsel you with My eye upon you. (Psalm 32:8)

Show me how to live my life according to Your will and the mission You have set before me, loving God.

Friends for Life

Ruby Dell Gracy knew Joyce Morgan was her best friend. But until it mattered most she didn't realize how seriously Joyce took that role.

When Gracy's three sons became ill with a congenital kidney ailment, she faced a desperate search for kidney donors for all of them. It was Morgan who, without hesitation, donated a kidney to Gracy's most seriously ill son.

The words "friendship" and "friend" signify a serious relationship. Do you and your friends enrich and improve each other's lives? Help and support each other?

A friend is indeed a rare and special gift, one who should be regarded and treated as such.

A true friend sticks closer than one's nearest kin. (Proverbs 18:24)

Jesus, true friends are loyal and courageous and put others' needs ahead of their own. Help me be an exemplary friend.

Act for Yourself

Most of us have had the experience of having somebody treat us badly—and then of responding in kind.

Not only do we wind up angry with the other person, but also annoyed with ourselves for speaking and behaving in a way that makes us ashamed of ourselves.

Sidney Harris, the longtime newspaper columnist and cartoonist, told the story of how a friend handled such a situation. The two of them had stopped at a newsstand where the owner was extremely rude and disparaging to Harris's friend. But the man was polite, even friendly to the vendor. After they walked away, Harris asked how he had stayed so pleasant and calm.

The man said, "Because I don't want him to decide how I am going to act. I am an actor, not a reactor."

Don't let someone else determine your attitude or actions. Rather than reacting, act for yourself.

Let us choose what is right. (Job 34:4)

Help me to always be my best self, Jesus. Show me how to imitate You in all things.

Forming Teams, Not Gangs

Sierra Vista Elementary School in Reno, Nevada, was filled with children ripe for recruiting by local gangs.

Then along came Mario Mendez. A teacher's assistant, he promoted discipline and self-esteem and filled after-school hours with positive activity by starting the school's first soccer league.

Mendez wanted the sport to be free, so he financed it by selling ice pops and candy. He built alliances with the police, who purchased equipment. His own wife Rosalba cooked meals for the team and even washed uniforms.

Sierra Vista's team took second place in its first year. But these kids are not only winners on the field, but also in the classroom. Before any of the 40 players participate in a practice or game, Mendez checks that homework is done.

A path to a better future all around began as a cure for gang membership. How will you help others find the right path?

Help the weak. (1 Thessalonians 5:14)

Help educators guide children into happy, successful, constructive, law-abiding lives, Jesus.

Creativity: Inside Out

If you find yourself admiring people who have a flair for creativity and would like to nurture your own, you can. Here are some ideas from researcher E. Paul Torrance:

1. Improvisation. When you face a challenge without an established method for dealing with it, draw on both your experience and your imagination.

2. Planned discovery. Focus on a particular idea, gather needed resources, consider various possibilities and refine your results until they're useful.

3. Self-expression. Seek inspiration. Listen to your intuition, explore mistakes and success. Use all the assets at your disposal—and, most of all, within yourself.

While some people may find that creative thinking comes more easily than do others, we all have the opportunity to develop our God-given powers. Have the courage to think things through—and then try something fresh and new. You just might surprise yourself.

There came a sound like the rush of a violent wind, and...all of them were filled with the Holy Spirit. (Acts 2:2,4)

Breathe Your life into me, Spirit of Counsel. Open my being to Your insight.

The Family That Plays Together...

If the demands of modern living have your family members running in different directions, maybe it's time for some fun and games.

Some families are rebelling against the retreat to a personal computer, television, DVD or audio player for solo entertainment.

According to an article in *U.S. News & World Report,* "yard games of all sorts are making a comeback. Aficionados say the sports allow social time outdoors and low key competition that favors neither young nor old, male nor female."

One game long popular with Italian immigrants in the U.S. is bocce, an ancient Roman game in which players toss balls as close as they can to a smaller marker ball known as the pallino. Bocce appears to be catching on. At least one high-end catalog, *Christopher's Games of Quality & Distinction,* offers a classy set.

Introduce yourself and your family to the simple pleasures of badminton, bocce or horseshoes.

The streets of the city shall be full of boys and girls playing. (Zechariah 8:5)

Thank You, Creator, for those precious times when children and adults, family and friends can play together.

Builders of Peace and Friendship

If Laila Najjar and Adi Frish had not lived in an "Oasis of Peace" they would never have become best friends.

Najjar, a Palestinian Muslim, and Frish, an Israeli Jew, grew up in a village known to Jews as Neve Shalom and to Palestinians as Wahat al-Salam, that was created in Israel in the 1970's. The English translation, "Oasis of Peace" describes the intent of the founders—for people of different backgrounds, enemies elsewhere, to live in harmony.

It has not always been easy for the young women, now in their 20's, especially when Frish fulfilled her required military service. But their relationship survived. Najjar told her friend, "I don't necessarily want to know about the Israeli army, Adi, but I always want to know about you."

Frish believes that "to have peace, we have to understand the other side better. We need to communicate and listen."

That's true for all people in all situations.

This is My covenant with you...no longer shall your name be Abram, but your name shall be Abraham; for I have made you the ancestor of a multitude of nations. (Genesis 17:4,5)

God of Abraham, You want Your children to live in respect-filled peace. Remind us that we are truly brothers and sisters.

Raise Your Voice in Praise to God

"We come from varying backgrounds and different church traditions, but we are united in song as we join voices in praise."

That's what retired Baptist pastor Rev. Harold Lang said at one of the monthly "hymn sings" he leads at a Presbyterian home for seniors in Inver Grove Heights, Minnesota.

"Decades ago this wouldn't have happened," believes Earl Ryan, one of the residents. He's happy that people who may never have set foot in churches of other denominations now sing and pray together.

Ellen Capecchi, a Catholic chaplain who helps organize the events, comments on the singers: "Here sits one who lost his vision this week; another who buried his spouse last month. There's one facing major surgery; another undergoing cancer treatment. Despite disability, disease or death, they sing out, united in praise."

Unite with others in your home, your church, your community, to praise God and to pray to Him.

Sing to the Lord a new song, His praise in the assembly of the faithful. ...praise His name with dancing, making melody to Him with tambourine and lyre. (Psalm 148:1,3)

Father and Creator of all, we worship You.

Living as a Child of God

In 1996, the Ku Klux Klan held a rally in Ann Arbor, Michigan, to spread their message of racial divisiveness. At the same time about 300 counter demonstrators had also gathered and the two groups converged in angry confrontation.

One of the Klan speakers in particular attracted the animosity of the crowd, which began to beat and kick the man. Suddenly a 19-year-old black woman, Keshia Thomas, threw herself on top of the Klansman to protect him.

The crowd fell back at the sight of her courageous and selfless act. Later, when asked why she risked her life for someone who stood for so much she opposed, Keshia Thomas said, simply, "He's still somebody's child."

Anger, hatred and fear can make us do things we might never have believed ourselves capable of doing. But, then, so can love. Love of God, of neighbor, and, yes, of ourselves, can keep us true to God's will for us.

See that none of you repays evil for evil, but always seek to do good to one another and to all. (1 Thessalonians 5:15)

Help me understand that I am Your child, Beloved Father. And that all my neighbors are Your children as well.

Wisdom at Work

Experience in the workplace teaches many lessons. Yet wise workers know that the simplest advice is often the best. These thoughts from *The Manager's Intelligence Report* bear repeating:

- "Don't be afraid of the phrase, 'I don't know.'" Don't try to bluff. If you made a mistake, accept the blame.
- "Never gossip." When someone gossips, two careers are hurt—the person being talked about, and the person talking.
- "No task is beneath you." Don't think you are above anything. Be a good example and pitch in.
- "Ask for help." If you think you're in over your head, you are. Ask someone to lend a hand.
- "When you don't like someone, don't let it show." Never burn bridges or offend others.
- "Let it go." When someone angers or disappoints you, don't harbor a grudge. Be gracious and move on.

Whatever your job, do your best with a happy heart.

Commit your work to the Lord. (Proverbs 16:3)

Work beside me, with me, Carpenter of Nazareth.

Healing Art

Sexual, physical and psychological abuse can produce life-long scars. Yet some survivors are finding their self-esteem through art.

The InnerArt Victory Exhibit at the ArtServe Gallery in Fort Lauderdale, Florida, displayed the work of 37 artists of all ages who survived some form of abuse.

"Through art, you're able to say, 'This is what I've been through and this is how I feel about it'," said Melanie Holcomb. "Art can heal by leaps and bounds." One of her works, titled "Caught," shows a woman trapped and tangled in a spider web.

Once victimized herself, Holcomb works for an agency which helps children in abusive situations.

Another artist abused in childhood began "painting before (she) could speak." That's how she survived. She now teaches art to children and finds it therapeutic. Art takes "anger and negative feelings away from the self."

What can you do to prevent abuse or to bring hope to the abused?

Take care that you do not despise one of these little ones...their angels continually see the face of My Father in heaven. (Matthew 18:10)

God, teach us to respect the physical, sexual and psychological integrity of children and adults.

Follow Your Passion

Is there a cause or issue about which you feel passionate?

Rather than waiting for someone else to tackle it, be the person who ignites change. It's often not as daunting as it seems.

Follow your passion. Think about what you care about most – children, people with a particular illness, the environment, your community. A burning desire to effect change is often the best fuel to sustain a long-term effort.

Evaluate your resources. Consider what you yourself can offer, be it time, talent or money, and then seek support from others.

Start small. Rather than trying to save the entire world, begin with one person in need. Tutoring just one person in English as a second language, for example, could launch a more organized, wider-scale effort.

'Come to Me, all you that are weary and are carrying heavy burdens, and I will give you rest.' (Matthew 11:28)

When I am discouraged or overwhelmed be my strength, Jesus. Remind me that with You anything is possible.

Facing an Ethical Dilemma

Have you ever been asked to do something dishonest at work? Whether it's a fellow employee, a customer or your boss who wants you to cheat, the problem can be a tough one.

Eric Harvey and Scott Airitam, authors of *Ethics 4 Everyone,* offer this three-part plan:

1. Explain your concern. Rather than attacking the other person, make an "I" statement: "I have doubts about the plan because...I think we need to find a different solution."

2. Offer an alternative. Suggest an ethical way to reach the objective. For example: "We both want to make a profit, and we can do it by cutting extra features rather than using substandard materials."

3. Ask for agreement. Be sure you both agree to proceed honestly. Try saying: "I need your help to get this done. Are we agreed on what we're going to do?"

Have the courage to stand up for honesty and moral values.

Birds roost with their own kind, so honesty comes home to those who practice it. (Sirach 27:9)

Spirit of Fortitude, grant me the wisdom and wit to choose always what is right, just and honorable.

Partying in Silence

One Saturday night in 2002, friends Tony Noe and Paul Rebhan entered a bar for a drink and a chat. But, as is often the case, the noise was too loud for conversation.

Later that year, the friends decided to offer an alternative. They played hosts at their first "quiet party." Guests scribble notes or images to each other using pen and paper instead of talking. Fans laud the trend as a means of quelling inane small talk and escaping the often ear-splitting cacophony of 21st century life.

Noe and Rebhan now offer starter kits for those who want to host their own silent soirées.

Every day, we need to make time, to take time, to tune out, so we can tune in to what—and Who—really matters.

Be silent before the Lord God! (Zephaniah 1:7)

In the stillness and silence, I listen for Your voice, Master.

Getting to "No" You

Ever feel so overwhelmed by your own "To Do" list that you could simply cry?

In a poignant essay, writer Ramona Cramer Tucker describes a time in her life when she was "stressed-out by life's demands, many self-induced." The answer, she concluded, was simply to say "no" more often and to prioritize her life.

"Saying 'yes' rolled off my tongue so easily, that 'no' seemed cumbersome," she explains. However, she managed to take charge of her schedule, her time and her life.

As Tucker puts it, "God hadn't created me to run around constantly 'chasing the wind,'" she says, citing Ecclesiastes 1:14.

Have everyday chores and tasks taken the joy out of living for you? Pare down your activities so you can get busy living.

I saw all the deeds that are done under the sun; and see, all is vanity and a chasing after the wind. (Ecclesiastes 1:14)

Jesus, carpenter from Nazareth, the business of living should not interfere with the joy of life. Enable me to direct my daily activities, instead of allowing them to direct me.

A Word to the Wise

What's the best advice a parent can give a child?

Surely there are many bits of wisdom that can smooth the way for youngsters as they mature into adults. Here are a few simple, but significant ideas from Brenda Player of South Carolina, writing in *Bits & Pieces.*

- Bitter words unspoken are never regretted.
- Don't get frustrated, get determined.
- Preserve family—it's one of the most important things on earth.
- Don't be judgmental. Realize that we will be judged by the same measuring stick by which we judge others.
- Be tolerant of people of other races, religions, beliefs, creeds or anything that makes them different from us. Remember that they are trying to be tolerant of us, too.

Even the best advice means nothing unless it's accepted—and followed. Think about what's really vital in your life and relationships and resolve to do your best.

Get wisdom; get insight. (Proverbs 4:5)

Guide me in wisdom and understanding, Holy Spirit. May I grow in maturity, whatever my age.

The Power to Inspire

Famous men and women find they have great power to influence and inspire huge numbers of people.

Cycling champ and stage-4 testicular cancer survivor Lance Armstrong raises money through the Lance Armstrong Foundation to help those diagnosed with cancer. LAF promotes the idea that knowledge is power and attitude is everything when dealing with cancer.

One recent project was the "Wear Yellow, Live Strong" campaign. Hundreds of yellow wristbands were sold to both ordinary people and celebrities.

Why yellow? Armstrong chose it because, as the color of the leader's jersey in the Tour de France bike race, it symbolizes "hope, courage, inspiration and perseverance."

Every one has power, locally or worldwide, to inspire. Use yours to encourage the good.

Provoke one another to love and good deeds. (Hebrews 10:24)

Remind us, Lord, that in helping others we serve You.

Family Fun

Facing a long cold winter's night? Do you want to have family fun and togetherness without television? Try word games. Here's one: come up with two words with the same spelling, but different pronunciation and meanings.

The bandage was wound around the wound.

The farm was used to produce produce.

The dump was so full that it had to refuse more refuse.

The insurance was invalid for the invalid.

There was a row among the oarsmen about how to row.

Upon seeing the tear in the painting I shed a tear.

After a number of injections, my jaw became number.

Discover more examples, then go on to other word games. Besides providing fun and togetherness, words games sharpen language skills and teach fair play. Try them. Enjoy them.

Do not deprive yourself of a day's enjoyment; do not let your share of desired good pass by you. (Sirach. 14:14)

God, help family members enjoy each other's company.

A Voice Returned

Sarah Scantlin was 18 when she was run down by a drunk driver. The brain-damaged woman hadn't spoken in two decades when she uttered her first words in early 2005.

No one knows why Sarah, who had been silent in a hospital under the watch of doctors and her family since the 1984 accident, suddenly recovered her ability to speak. She simply answered her nurse one day, and then asked to speak to her parents. Her memory has begun to recover, as well.

Doctors suspect that vital pathways in Sarah's brain had regenerated, allowing her to speak and remember. And though Sarah will never fully recover from the accident, and will most likely have to remain in the hospital, her family is thrilled.

"She's 100 percent Sarah again," her father said. "It's simply a joyous situation."

Even the bleakest of circumstances can yield happy surprises. Always trust in hope.

Hope for good things, for lasting joy and mercy. (Sirach 2:9)

Lord, help me to remain steadfast in a challenging world.

Thinking about "What If"

If you had it to do over again, what would you do differently?

That's what a study asked 50 people over the age of 90. Sociologist Tony Campolo found that while there many answers, three ideas came up over and over again. Here's what the participants said:

- I would reflect more.
- I would risk more.
- I would do more things that would live on after me.

There's a lot to be said for each point. By reflecting more, we can contemplate what is really important to us. By risking more, we can use opportunities to turn dreams into realities. By getting involved with something bigger than ourselves, we can make a difference in this world of ours.

While we can't live our lives over again, we can live every day with zest, with meaning, with purpose. And we can start right this minute.

I came that they may have life, and have it abundantly. (John 10:10)

Eternal Father, show me how to be the whole and holy person You created me to be.

An Act of Hope

She's played roles on the big and small screens, but to foster children in her home state of Mississippi, Sela Ward's best acting part is as their hero.

In 2001, when the actress learned there was no place in Mississippi for foster children who hadn't found permanent homes, she formed the Hope Village Foundation. She purchased an old orphanage on 30 acres in Meridian and turned it into Hope Village for Children. Up to 32 children, from newborns to teenagers are housed in three cottages with siblings kept together. The children can stay until they turn 18.

Ward spends a month in Meridian each summer, and visits the Village throughout the year.

When faced with a challenge or a need for a change, it is best to begin with a heart full of love–and hope.

Rescue the oppressed, defend the orphan, plead for the widow. (Isaiah 1:17)

Lord, lead me to where I can best reflect Your love.

What Did You Just Say?

Every parent can remember the first time his or her toddler (or older child) said a word that froze everyone in the room into stunned silence. At some point, every mom or dad has had to play "language cop."

What's a parent to do? According to one writer, there are degrees of infraction when it comes to vulgar words: "stupid" is somewhat benign compared to swear words and should be treated as such.

Perhaps the best suggestion comes from a writer who says she reminds her kids of the "D" word when they speak inappropriately: disrespect. "While it's important to focus on single words," she suggests, "it's just as important to look at their whole context."

Take care with every word you speak. Words spoken cannot be "taken back," even with an apology.

Where there is no whisperer, quarreling ceases. (Proverbs 26:20)

Help me avoid gossip and to walk away when others gossip, Merciful Savior.

Teens Care for Others

Teen volunteers are welcome at the Westminster Free Clinic in Westlake Village, California, northwest of Los Angeles.

Every week the clinic opens its doors to the poor, uninsured and homeless people of the area. When the daughter of an adult volunteer offered her help several years ago, Dr. Steve Kamajian decided it could be useful for both the clinic and young people. Under the supervision of a nurse, teens record medical histories, take vital signs—and get a close-up look at health care careers.

Michelle Levy, who hopes to be a physician someday, feels "rewarded to know that I am helping patients who would otherwise not have access to health care. And I feel humbled by the graciousness and gratitude of the people who come to the clinic."

Good health care is vital to everyone. Look after your neighbors' well-being as a matter of both compassion and social justice.

A man was going down from Jerusalem to Jericho...a Samaritan...was moved with pity... bandaged his wounds...and took care of him. (Luke 10:30,33,34)

Blessed Creator, who loves each of us so much, inspire me to care for my neighbors in need, as well as my loved ones and myself.

Creating Sibling Solidarity

Any parent of two or more children knows how intense and hurtful sibling rivalry can be. How can parents turn "sibling rivalry" into "sibling solidarity"? Try these tips for peace.

See the big picture. Too often grownups step in at the "shriek stage" of a conflict, and haven't seen what prompted that extreme reaction. Observe the children at play. Encourage good behavior.

Focus on feelings. Nothing is solved or resolved in anger. Try calm down techniques before any major discussions.

Rely on rules. Children count on your setting limits.

Let kids own the answer. Help children come to their own solutions.

Model good behavior. Promote teachable moments in family activities, such as playing board games that promote cooperation.

Helping siblings get along will go a long way in ensuring that they get along with spouses and others later in life.

Is not this the carpenter's son? Is not His mother called Mary? Are not His brothers... and...His sisters with us? (Matthew 13:55,56)

We give thanks, God, that we are brothers and sisters, united by the love of one Lord.

Trees of Peace

Nobel peace laureate Wangari Maathai chose an unusual method of promoting peace and meeting the needs of the impoverished: planting trees.

Maathai perceived an inextricable link between the environment and world peace, particularly in rural communities in her native Kenya. In her opinion, good governance observes sound environmental practices, and as she says, when natural resources are degraded or exploited, violence is more likely to erupt among these isolated communities.

What began as a simple effort providing firewood to rural women in Kenyan villages grew to a widespread campaign to plant more than 30,000 trees in Kenya alone. Now a member of Kenya's Parliament, she has attracted worldwide attention to her many causes.

Maathai offers the unique example of how one seedling of hope can lead to a multitude of solutions. What ideas do you have that could use some nurturing?

They are like trees planted by streams of water, which yield their fruit in season. (Psalm 1:3)

Help me bring my ideas to fruition, my thoughts to action, Lord of the harvest.

Doctor on Duty

Dr. Todd Coulter of Ocean Springs, Mississippi, is one of a handful of physicians who have sworn off medical insurance. Instead, he has a thriving practice charging a flat rate of $40 a visit.

Midway Family Care is open six days a week. Dr. Coulter aims to provide affordable healthcare that will allow him a decent living at the same time. He says that patients are pleased: "The response has been phenomenal. This removes the financial fear of seeking medical care."

The doctor is also active in the community and his church. He believes he lives his vocation in his work everyday.

"It's a call to serve," says Dr. Coulter. "It's a chance to lead. If you accept the idea of the ministerial priesthood of Jesus Christ, you accept the idea that no matter what we do in life we're all called."

Open yourself to the service of your neighbor.

**Honor physicians for their services.
(Sirach 38:1)**

Almighty God, grant me the desire to help my brothers and sisters each day of my life.

Too Old to Try Something New?

If you think that you have waited too long to go back to school, switch careers or learn new skills, think again. Here are a few people who had major achievements late in life:

- George Burns won his Oscar at 80.
- Golda Meir became prime minister of Israel at 71.
- Albert Schweitzer was still performing surgery in his African hospital at 89.
- S.I. Hayakawa retired as president of San Francisco State University at 70 and then won election to the U.S. Senate.
- Grandma Moses started painting when she was 80 and continued after she was 100.

However many years God gives us, let's make each one count. And, for that matter, each day, as well.

Remember your Creator in the days of your youth, before the days of trouble come, and the years...when you will say, "I have no pleasure in them." (Ecclesiastes 12:1)

Thank You, Divine Lord for the time and talent You have given me to be of service to You and Your children.

When Getting Better Is a Laughing Matter

Robert Schimmel grew up watching the "greats" of comedy. "I learned that if you could make people laugh, everyone liked you," he said.

Later in his life, Schimmel discovered that the power of laughter would help him—and others.

Diagnosed with cancer in 2000, the stand-up comedian found himself facing chemotherapy. "I started bringing comedy CDs with me to the clinic," he said. "I loaned my CDs to other patients, and pretty soon, they were laughing too."

"When you're diagnosed with cancer, you start to bargain with God: 'Let me get through this, and I'll learn to live every day to the fullest,'" he observed. "Isn't it sad that you have to get sick before giving yourself permission to live life to the fullest?"

Today, Schimmel continues to live a full life—even welcoming a son in 2003. Life is best faced with a smile.

You are safe. Be strong and courageous. (Daniel 10:19)

Master, source of all hope and joy, I give thanks for the blessings You send my way.

Popcorn Power

Much like Girl Scouts and their more famous cookies, Boy Scouts often sell popcorn to raise funds. What most Boy Scouts don't do, however, is sell over 10 tons of the stuff.

But Ryan Cenk did just that, raising $25,006. He cinched the record of the most Boy Scout popcorn ever sold when he pitched his wares to a family friend who happened to be the vice-president of a financial firm. Deciding that tins of popcorn would make great gifts for his employees, the family friend bought $13,500 worth.

Trail's End, the company that produces the popcorn sold in Boy Scout drives, rewarded Ryan for his sales savvy by treating him to a trip to Disney World. The company also invited him to speak at their annual sales meeting.

Hard work and innovative thinking can produce great success. How can you apply those tools to your own projects?

Human success is in the hand of the Lord. (Sirach 10:5)

Lord, help me never to settle for the ordinary.

Sowing Seeds of Hope

It started with just three gardens, part of Bethel Lutheran Church's effort to help needy families help themselves.

Now every February, members of Bethel Lutheran distribute bags of seeds for over 200 vegetable and fruit gardens. One year, 560 individuals were fed from 176 of these gardens.

Canning equipment is also provided, so food can be stockpiled for the winter. The materials are handed out at Bethel, and seven food banks and a nonprofit center nearby.

Helping others help themselves—offering a means to autonomy and greater self esteem—takes creativity and effort, but it is the greatest gift any one can give.

Encourage one another. (1 Thessalonians 4:18)

Lord, help me this day to encourage at least one other person gain independence and grow in self-esteem.

The Benefit of the Doubt

Has anyone ever told you an utterly unbelievable story–that just happened to be true?

Broker Michael Guess was in his investment office in Tennessee when a disheveled woman named Alice Perley entered saying she had an account. She was vague, but she said she had investments with the firm, possibly through an out-of-state branch.

Thinking she was homeless, Guess offered her some money, but Perley politely refused, saying she was a client. So he checked her story with the Atlanta office. It was true. And her family had been seeking her ever since a breakdown she had had eight years earlier. By the next day they were reunited.

The broker, who had made an effort to listen and to suspend his disbelief, said simply, "We're supposed to remember to help one another and not just walk on by–aren't we?"

Yes. We are.

Let anyone with ears to hear listen! (Luke 8:8)

I expect people to listen to me willingly and wholeheartedly, Spirit of Wisdom. Help me do the same.

Making the Most of Music

When you are stopped in your tracks by a problem, do you solve it by doing the logical thing? Or do you try to do even better?

Years ago, while violinist Itzhak Perlman was giving a concert one of the violin's strings broke. The sudden snap was heard by everyone in the hall; the other musicians stopped playing.

Rather than have the string replaced, Perlman took a few moments to collect himself and then signaled the conductor to pick up where they had left off. The great musician used the three remaining strings to finish the performance.

When the audience gave him a standing ovation, Perlman addressed them, saying, "Sometimes it is the artist's task to find out how much music you can make with what you have left."

Don't let any struggle or setback stop you from making music with your life.

It is good to...sing praises to Your Name, O Most High; to declare Your steadfast love...to the music of the lute and the harp. (Psalm 92:1,2,3)

Ever-loving Lord, teach my spirit to sing and to soar with Yours.

Mama, I Want To Read

Thelma Harrison didn't retreat when she retired. After decades as a nurse and civil rights activist in New York City, Harrison retired to her hometown of Norfolk, Virginia and turned her humanitarian impulses toward children.

As an octogenarian great-great-grandmother, Harrison became a finalist in the Volvo for Life Awards for her work as volunteer director of "Mama, I Want To Read," the program she founded after retiring.

The free summer program helps prepare three and four-year-olds for kindergarten by teaching them counting, ABCs and basics such as how to tie their shoes and remember their phone numbers.

"She's a sainted figure around here," said Norfolk Public Schools grant writer Gary Ruegsegger, who nominated Harrison. "Her greatest love in life is helping others to help themselves."

Consider the ways an active retirement might not only help you, but others as well.

How attractive is sound judgment...good counsel ...wisdom...understanding and...rich experience (in)...the aged. (Sirach 25:4,5)

Increase our respect for the wisdom and dignity of aged women and men, Jesus.

A Dream Fulfilled

Dr. Tom Virnig was a good son to his parents for 29 years, a loving husband for 10 months and a physician for one day.

Despite his terminal illness, Dr. Virnig never gave up on his dream to become a doctor. His struggle with leukemia, diagnosed in his third year of medical school, never derailed him from his plans or his optimism.

Amidst chemotherapy, kidney dialysis and a bone marrow transplant, he persevered. And on the very day before his death, he received the reward for all his toil: hearing someone call him "Doctor Virnig."

No admirable effort is ever in vain. Pursuing one's dream is often a reward in itself.

Happy are those who persevere. (Daniel 12:12)

Lord God, inspire the discouraged. Remind each of us that You stand with us through every trial, test and challenge.

Overwhelmed by Kindness

After a man wielding a sawed-off shotgun smashed his way into their Florida home, two women kept their cool and overpowered the intruder—with kindness.

Cathy Ord, 60, and Rose Bucher, 63, offered the man a ham sandwich with pickles, a bottle of rum and a shower, even providing him with a disposable razor to shave off his scruffy beard. They also chatted with him, agreeing to call him a taxi when he indicated he was ready to leave.

But when the well-fed "guest" fell asleep while awaiting the cab, the two women called the police who came and arrested the man. The homeless intruder was charged with home invasion and false imprisonment.

Sometimes our greatest weapons in the face of hatred and hostility—even danger—are love and kindness.

If your enemies are hungry, feed them; if...thirsty, give them something to drink; for by doing this you will heap burning coals on their heads. (Romans 12:20)

Father, protect the elderly.

The Best Letter You Never Sent

Have you ever wanted to send a harsh letter to someone who had treated you badly? We usually either wind up not doing it and brooding about it, or we send one and make the situation worse.

Abraham Lincoln had another approach. When his Secretary of War, Edwin Stanton was angered by an army officer who accused him of favoritism, Lincoln told Stanton to write a strong letter. Stanton did, and showed it to Lincoln, who asked, "What are you going to do with it now?"

When Stanton said he intended to mail it, Lincoln replied: "You don't want to send that letter. Put it in the stove. That's what I do when I've written a letter when I'm angry or bitter. It's a good letter and you had a good time writing it, and feel better now. Go ahead, burn it, and write another letter with less sharp edges."

Try choosing words with "less sharp edges."

With the judgment you make you will be judged, and the measure you give will be the measure you get. (Matthew 7:2)

Jesus, show me how to treat others the way I would want to be treated and the way I would treat You.

Popeye's Wedding Invitation

As the cartoonist for the "Popeye" comic strip, Hy Eisman breathes life into the gruff, squinty-eyed sailor with the bulging forearms every week.

Unlike his pen-and-ink alter ego, Eisman, 78, is quiet, even shy. When his wife of 42 years died of cancer in the fall of 1997, Eisman quickly retreated into a shell.

Then he met Florence Greenberg in the Englewood, New Jersey, public library as she looked through the how-to books. Greenberg's husband had died in the summer of the same year Eisman had lost his wife.

After their initial meeting, the two shared coffee and "instantly felt a connection," both said. Three years later, the couple sent out wedding invitations–a folded comic strip with Popeye and Olive Oyl announcing their upcoming nuptials.

Even when life seems as black-and-white–and bleak–as newsprint, love can come calling–filling your world with color!

If I speak in the tongues of mortals and of angels ...if I have prophetic powers...and all knowledge ...all faith...but do not have love, I am nothing. (1 Corinthians 13:1,2)

Loving Jesus, remind us that you know our deep need for love.

Celebrating St. Valentine's Day

Celebrate, with more than the usual chocolates, flowers, cards, champagne and dinners in restaurants. Celebrate your heart.

Let go of old arguments and resentments.

Be young at heart. Watch clouds pass—see any animal shapes? Describe the colors. Spend a day at the zoo.

Remind yourself of all the wonderful things that have happened to you; your successes.

Find a friend after your own heart. Then share—and listen to your friend's—most intimate thoughts, desires and fears.

Care for your heart. Know your blood pressure and cholesterol numbers. If they are high, work with your doctor to improve them and your overall health.

You—and your loved ones—need your heart to be tender and human; and to beat for many years. So does God.

A new heart I will give you, and a new spirit I will put within you; and I will remove from your body the heart of stone and give you a heart of flesh. (Ezekiel 36:26)

Jesus, make my heart a compassionate and loving heart; a healthy heart.

A Light Shines Through

Paul Rusesabagina never thought of himself as an idealistic man. Yet when an outbreak of genocidal violence engulfed his native Rwanda in 1994, he took a stand.

Radical Hutus had begun to slaughter their neighboring Tutsis, people who shared the same language and culture. Soon, they were also killing moderate Hutus who refused to participate in the 100 days of violence that ultimately claimed over 800,000 lives.

Rusesabagina, a Hutu, turned the hotel he managed into an impromptu refugee camp. Using every ounce of influence he had and calling in every favor he was owed, he did all he could to ensure the safety of his family and the over 1,000 people who turned to him for help. Ten years later, Rusesabagina's story was dramatized in the film *Hotel Rwanda,* which was recognized with a 2005 Christopher Award.

When things are most desperate, then a person's goodness can shine most brightly.

The good person out of the good treasure of the heart produces good. (Luke 6:45)

Lord, help me to find my innate strength and bravery when I need it.

A Mini-Sensation

In early 2005, the artist Christo oversaw the building of thousands of frames holding saffron-colored drapes in New York's Central Park. His project, *The Gates,* drew thousands of sightseers and worldwide media attention.

As a joke, Geoff Hargadon of Somerville, Massachusetts, constructed several miniature versions of *The Gates* and arranged them throughout his house. Christening himself "Hargo," he put photos of *The Somerville Gates* on his website.

What Hargadon didn't expect was that over 4 million people would visit his site in just a few days. Galleries across the country asked to display his work. The mayor of Somerville even declared an official "Hargo Day" in his honor.

"It's been so overwhelming," Hargadon said. "It touched people on a whole variety of levels." Unexpectedly, Hargadon had pleased everyone from art enthusiasts to those who just wanted a good laugh.

Whatever you do touches others. Isn't that incentive enough to always give your best, no matter what?

**I wholeheartedly followed the Lord.
(Joshua 14:8)**

Holy Lord, may I give my all to all I do.

Passionate about Music

A number of well-trained Chinese performers have traveled far and sacrificed much in hopes of introducing traditional Chinese music to a wider audience.

"I want to try my luck in New York," said Zhisheng Zhang, a descendant of Chinese court musicians, who plays a type of multipiped mouth organ called a sheng. "In China serious artists like us aren't as respected as pop singers."

While he dreams of someday appearing in one of New York City's great concert halls, he sets up his own small performance space on various subway platforms. "I love...playing the sheng. It's in my blood."

Many fear that the music from China's 5,000 year-old civilization is being edged out by Western-style music. Zhang and his fellow musicians are trying to counter this trend.

Find your passion. Pursue it enthusiastically.

Let us now sing the praises of...those who composed musical tunes, or put verses in writing. (Sirach 44:1,5)

Inspire musicians to persevere in their studies and practice, and to use their gifts to glorify You, Creator.

Hopeful Sounds

Marli Spieker uses her radio programs to broadcast messages of hope and encouragement to oppressed women wherever her voice can reach them throughout the world.

According to Spieker, she was motivated to help after seeing cultural and religious injustices in her travels. She directs her attention to women who are viewed as property (some forced into prostitution), or barred from education and employment.

Spieker is founder and executive director of Project Hannah, whose radio programs have both practical and spiritual aspects. The "lessons for your life" segment covers such day-to-day matters as good nutrition and stress management; while "lessons for your soul" is Spieker's effort to share with her audience the eternal hope which sustains her.

"We not only have to teach them how to receive eternal life, but also how to live a better life."

God created humankind in His image...male and female He created them. (Genesis 1:27)

Help us respect all women and girls for their God-given dignity and intelligence, Spirit of Wisdom.

Gifts that Give

Leslie Ligon's son was born blind. But she and her husband wanted him to learn Braille, the language of touch, as one way to a full life.

Ligon also decided to "promote Braille literacy within the blind and sighted communities by offering fun, reasonably priced fashion jewelry for everyone." She began At First Sight jewelry.

"By playing upon the visual elements of Braille, I hope to introduce the lyrical quality of it to people who've known nothing about it." At First Sight jewelry has produced Braille heart pendants for Valentine's Day, Braille alphabet bracelets, rings, crosses and necklaces.

A percentage of her earnings is donated to organizations promoting Braille literacy.

Gifts given and received can have many unforeseen benefits. Consider giving gifts that give more.

(Jesus) spat on the ground and made mud with the saliva and spread the mud on the man's eyes, saying to him, "Go, wash in the pool of Siloam." (John 9:6-7)

We are all blind in one way or another, Divine Physician. Help us to be patient with each other's blindness.

Can This Language Be Saved?

It's not a language most people could speak or understand. Yet, Allen Sockabasin has spent more than a decade trying to keep the Native American Passamaquoddy or Maliseet language alive.

Fewer than 600 people in the Passamaquoddys' indigenous lands, eastern Maine and adjacent Canada, speak their ancestral language. Still, Sockabasin's goal is to educate enough Passamaquoddys in the basics of their language that they will be able to pray in it.

Sockabasin, who grew up speaking Passamaquoddy, has translated spiritual songs and poems. "I know when I say 'my Creator' in my language, there is no other definition," he says. "It's who made me."

Preserving one's language and traditions can help us cope with the present. What traditions do you hold dear? How can you live their meaning and mystery?

Remember the wonderful works He has done, His miracles, and the judgments He uttered. (1 Chronicles 16:12)

God, ever ancient, ever new, help me glorify You.

Guidelines for Living

Finch College for Women does not exist anymore, but from 1900 until 1975 it welcomed many young New Yorkers with these guidelines for students that are still worth considering:

- Believing in people usually brings out the best in them.
- There is always another side; suspend judgment.
- Be considerate. Your actions affect others, and other people's feelings are just like your own.
- Be kind. Remember that other people are as intuitive as you are, and judge you just as you do them.
- Be sincere. In the long run everyone will find you out and judge you by your true self and not by your pretensions.
- Snobbishness of any kind is a sign of limitation.
- Remember that you have a soul just as you have a body and a social self. Do not starve it.

If the principles that guide your life are worthy, live up to them; if not, change them.

In great and small matters cause no harm. (Sirach 5:15)

Inspire my devotion to all that is good and to You, Lord.

Reading on the Rails

When officials of Mexico City's Metro (subway system) were looking to cut crime, they came up with a novel idea: free books.

Mariano Cruz, a Metro spokesman, said it was a way "to elevate and promote culture. We hope this can change attitudes and help people get along better."

The paperbacks contain short stories and poems from several authors. People pick them up at the stations and are asked to drop them off when they exit—on the honor system.

Police officer Heriberto Zigo believes it promotes honesty. He also says that reading quality literature is good for the character and gives commuters something in common to discuss.

Many passengers say that they cannot remember the last time anybody gave away anything or trusted strangers. Whether or not it reduces crime, the project is certainly creating good will.

Next time you have a problem, use your imagination.

The wise mind will know the time and way. (Ecclesiastes 8:5)

Help me to nurture both my honesty and my creativity, Holy Trinity.

The Place Where Children Grow

"It takes a lot of hands to heal these children," says Scott Hummel, who, with his wife Kathy, founded Our Little Haven in 1993 to serve abused, neglected and wounded children in the St. Louis area.

Children go there for many reasons: born prematurely with developmental needs from prenatal drug exposure; born HIV-positive; or abused after birth and having special medical needs.

"Broken bones can be dealt with," Hummel explains. "The real work comes in healing their broken hearts...helping them understand that they are loved, helping them to grow and live and learn and thrive, to feel nurtured and important."

The Hummels, and hundreds of volunteers, try to accomplish those goals. "Every day we offer our thanks and abandon our efforts to God's grace and thank Him for using us," the couple says.

How is God calling you to serve Him today?

"I have come to do Your will." (Hebrews 10:9)

Loving Lord, use me this day to serve someone in need.

Teaching Students to Speak Out

From watching TV crime dramas, you might think that forensics refers just to criminology. But there's another meaning: competitive public speaking or debate.

Tommie Lindsey, who teaches forensics at Logan High School, in Union City, California, knows its value. He says, "Speaking in public is... frightening to many people. ...But I believe that getting good at it can be the key to success."

That's true for his students, many of whom are minorities and poor. He spends his own time working with the youngsters, and has even bought them new clothes for their tournaments. Virtually all of them go on to four-year colleges and many become teachers, doctors and lawyers.

In 2004, Lindsey won a MacArthur Fellowship for his dedicated efforts. Yet his real goal is for his students "to go back and be a voice in their communities."

Be a voice for your community, especially for those who cannot speak for themselves.

Do not add to the troubles of the desperate, or delay giving to the needy...and give no one reason to curse you; for...their Creator will hear their prayer. (Sirach 4:3,5-6)

Let my words and deeds always express compassion for my neighbors, Spirit of God.

Simple Philosophy for a Little House

Laura Ingalls Wilder is famous for her *Little House* series of children's books. However, if it hadn't been for her own daughter, Rose, she might never have written them.

Rose Wilder Lane grew up to become a respected journalist. In the early 1930's, she begged her mother to write down the wonderful memories of her pioneer childhood in the upper Midwest of the 1870's which she had so often recounted. Lane became Wilder's agent, editor and collaborator.

Mother and daughter made an effort to see that each book was told from a child's viewpoint. The result was literature that's still popular.

Wilder believed in the basics: "It is still best to be honest and truthful; to make the most of what we have; to be happy with simple pleasures and to be cheerful and have courage when things go wrong."

That's a great philosophy for every life.

Revere the Lord, and serve Him in sincerity and in faithfulness. (Joshua 24:14)

Holy Spirit, remind me to delight in truth and simplicity.

Seeing Things Through

First it was his right eye. Everything went blurry for Hal McCoy, sports reporter for the *Dayton Daily News* in Ohio. A stroke of the optic nerve was the diagnosis.

For a man who needed his vision to report on ball games, the incident was a curve ball for his career and his coping skills. The odds were against it happening to his other eye, doctors said—but two years later, it did.

While McCoy faced many moments of wanting to quit, his editor, colleagues, players, and especially his wife Nadine pushed him to hang on—and he did.

"Sometimes I think my reporting has gotten better," he says. "Losing my eyesight has made me a better listener." McCoy's advice: "Don't ever give up on yourself. Don't ever give up on something you love."

Having vision means seeing life with a hope-filled mind and heart.

Moved with compassion, Jesus touched their eyes. Immediately they regained their sight and followed Him. (Matthew 20:34)

All around me I see the beauty of Your creation. For this, Lord, I praise You.

A Student's Best Friend

Every Friday at the Woodland Elementary Charter School in Georgia, a select group of students practice their reading skills by reading aloud to a willing listener such as a golden retriever.

As part of a special program overseen by a local veterinarian, Woodland helps children with physical disabilities practice and improve their reading skills with service dogs who sit, listen and show appreciation once the child is finished reading.

The program is said to have had remarkable success in helping the children's reading ability and self esteem. "When the dogs put their heads in the students' laps, it's very motivating and reassuring," says one school official.

All of God's creatures have a place in this, His world. Showing mercy and kindness is a way to honor the Creator of all.

Be merciful as your Father is merciful. (Luke 6:36)

Thank You for all the wondrous creatures You have made, Eternal Creator.

Humor in Speech

Some people enjoy "collecting" oxymorons or, as the *Oxford Pocket English Dictionary* defines them "figures of speech in which apparently contradictory terms appear together." Here are a few:

Found missing

Legally drunk

Genuine imitation

Good grief

Sweet sorrow

Same difference

Almost exactly

Silent scream

Working vacation

Clearly misunderstood

How we speak can be contradictory or direct; dishonest or honest. Honest, direct speech is best.

Let your word be 'Yes, Yes' or "No, No'; anything more...comes from the evil one. (Matthew 5:37)

Jesus, help us be truthful in speech as well as in deeds.

A Different Kind of Fasting

Lent is virtually synonymous with penance. As a time of preparation for the joy of the Resurrection, the glory of Easter, that's appropriate. But, fasting means more than eating less food.

Word Among Us magazine offered some ideas for expanding the concept of fasting:

- Fast from anger and hatred.
- Fast from judging others.
- Fast from discouragement.
- Fast from complaining.
- Fast from resentment or bitterness
- Fast from spending too much money.

All people can gain a great deal by giving up something to which they cling, whether a poor habit or a hurtful attitude. Today, give up one thing that distances you from others and from God.

This (is) the fast that I choose: to loose the bonds of injustice...to let the oppressed go free ...to share your bread with the hungry...when you see the naked, to cover them, and not to hide yourself from your own. (Isaiah 58:6,7)

Lord, grant me Your grace this Lent that I may grow in love for You and Your children—including myself.

Youngster Has a Modest Proposal

Can one youngster make a difference with one letter?

Ella Gunderson of Seattle did by telling a major department store chain she was unhappy with their too-revealing clothing. She wrote:

"Dear Nordstrom,

"I am an 11-year-old girl who has tried shopping at your store for clothes (in particular jeans), but all of them ride way under my hips, and the next size up is too big and falls down."

She went on to say that while the salesclerks suggest "that there is only one look. ...I think you should change that."

Two company executives wrote back, not only agreeing with her, but saying they would educate buyers and salespeople to insure a full range of fashion choices for young people.

Ella Gunderson's efforts gained media attention and the support of many of her peers as well as their parents.

If you have something important to say, say it.

Approval goes before one who is modest. (Sirach 32:10)

Holy Lord, encourage Your children, whatever their ages, to do what they believe to be right and good.

Cupid Cabbie

If you're single and traveling by cab in New York City, be on the lookout for cabbie Ahmed Ibrahim. He just might introduce you to your true love.

Ibrahim, who emigrated from Egypt 25 years ago, meets countless people while driving his taxi twelve hours a day. He realized early on that passengers often told hard luck stories, especially about their affairs of the heart.

So it occurred to Ibrahim that he might be able to help the lovelorn by matching them up with other passengers. He records interviews with interested parties and files it and their cell phone numbers. Then, when he meets a passenger who might make a good match, he connects them for a blind date. One happy participant exclaimed, "It was the best blind date of my life."

There's no charge for the service. He does it because he believes he can help people find happiness.

And you? How can you bring others happiness?

Overcome evil with good. (Romans 12:21)

Make me a bearer of goodwill, loving Lord.

The Wind beneath Their Wings

Chances are, you've heard of celebrated and talented performers such as Bette Midler, Ben Vereen and Tony Bennett. But have you heard of Helen Jordan?

Ironically, without Helen Jordan, you might never have heard from her now-famous students, including Midler, Vereen and Bennett. That's because Helen Jordan has spent most of her adult life behind the scenes, providing expert training, guidance and coaching to singers, musicians and performers, leading many of them to stardom.

At 98, she continues to enjoy the accolades and support of both her famous and not-so-famous student body. Says one former student, "Without Helen, I wouldn't have had the career I've had."

Who has helped guide your life and development? Take time to express your gratitude. Those who work to further the talents of others deserve appreciation, sincerely and often.

A disciple is not above the teacher, but everyone who is fully qualified will be like the teacher. (Luke 6:40)

Jesus, remind me to thank those who help me reach my goals. And show me how to extend a hand to others.

Faith and Hope on the Road

Lion Goodman, a traveling salesman, allowed a fellow traveler who was down on his luck to tag along, buying meals and even offering the man clothing.

On their third night together, the traveler unexpectedly shot Goodman four times. After the first shot, Goodman gave up his fears and surrendered his fate to God. "Love and light flowed through me," Goodman later recounted.

Goodman's assailant was stunned that his benefactor hadn't been killed. Riddled with doubt, he agreed to take Goodman to a hospital. Yet on the way, he stopped once more and again threatened to kill Goodman. Goodman's response was simple – he forgave his assailant.

Goodman's previous kindness, his uncanny will to survive and his benevolence were all too much for the man who would be his killer. He agreed to let Goodman go.

Hope and faith can see you through even the worst of circumstances.

Love your enemies, do good, and lend, expecting nothing in return. (Luke 6:35)

Lord, help me to find hope and faith when I need it.

Creatively Helping Those in Need

When one hears the phrase "homeless shelter," it's not likely that the image is one of comfort and security.

Genevieve Piturro and Alice Pagano knew that for most homeless children, nighttime often signifies a hard end to an even harder day. They knew that many of these children simply fell off to sleep in their street clothes...or nothing at all.

The two founded the Pajama Program, a not-for-profit organization that tries to make life for homeless children in a number of cities a bit cozier by collecting new and gently used pajamas for needy and abused children.

There are countless ways to help those in need. Use a little creativity in your quest to help others and it may lead to wonderful and fulfilling results.

Come, you that are blessed by My Father, inherit the kingdom...for I was naked and you gave me clothing. (Matthew 25:34,36)

Remind me to work harder to identify solutions, not just problems, Spirit of Understanding.

An Impressive History

How many businesses can boast an over 1,000 year history with more than seven centuries of continuous family ownership? In the small Italian town of Agnone, the Marinellis can.

Their remarkable, family-owned, church-bell making business has been going strong for centuries. The Marinellis have been delivering excellence in the ancient art of bell-making, with a workforce of 12 people today.

From the tiniest of bells in small village churches, to the six-ton bell hanging in the Vatican, to the Peace Bell at United Nations headquarters in New York, bells from the Marinelli foundry are heard worldwide.

Excellence takes patience, practice, but perhaps mostly time. Take time to explore and refine your own talents and gifts. You might be surprised at what could emerge.

The first...said, "Lord, your pound has made ten more pounds."...The second came saying, "Lord, your pound has made five pounds."...The other came saying, "Lord, here is your pound." (Luke 19:16,18,20)

Give me the patience, fortitude and discipline to nurture the talents You gave me, God.

The World of 'I'

What's the difference between a healthy love of self and self-absorption? Here's one description of the extremes of self-centeredness:

*"The world of 'I' is
a cozy place to be;
No one else lives there
but Myself and Me.
Me does what I bid,
Myself is Ego and Id,
and there's no room at all
for Them, They or Thee!"*

True love of self admits its own needs, but is responsive to the needs of others as well. At its best, love of self is a reflection of God's love. And if we keep God at the center of our lives, we will never have to worry about dwelling in a cold, sad, lonely world of 'I'—that we would only long desperately to escape.

Hear the commandments of life...give ear, and learn...where there is wisdom...strength... understanding...length of days and life...light for the eyes and peace. (Baruch 3:9,14)

Show me, Holy Trinity, how I can help satisfy the needs of my brothers and sisters, and fulfill myself.

The Double Bottom Line

Many MBA students become "visionaries who mix business acumen with a desire to distribute vaccines, educate low-income children or fight racism," according to a newspaper story.

These socially conscious students care about both bottom lines—the financial one and the "do-good" one.

"You could have a soup kitchen...where all the labor is volunteer and all the materials are donated—pure charity," says one faculty advisor. Or, you could have a for-profit company, with some social purpose.

Martin Curiel, with a masters in business Administration from Harvard, grew up in a migrant-farmer family hauling bags of peaches. He started the Migrant M.B.A. Project to help others go to business school or become entrepreneurs.

One professor's question—"How do you incorporate social values as well as economic values into decision-making?"—is both important and possible. Consider what you can do.

Better is a little with righteousness than large income with injustice. (Proverbs 16:8)

Inspire entrepreneurs to be honest, Holy Spirit.

A Farm Raises Hopes and Produce

The youngsters who work at the Added Value urban farm not only learn how to grow and sell organic produce they also learn skills of leadership and teamwork. And buyers who love locally grown eggplants, melons, cucumbers, snap peas, cabbages and tomatoes also benefit.

Ian Marvy, executive director and co-founder of the neighborhood non-profit, also hopes to "promote the sustainable development" of the Red Hook section of Brooklyn.

"Theirs is the best model in the United States," according to John Ameroso of the Cornell University Cooperative Extension program. Added Value "has built the farm from the asphalt up, raising a greenhouse, compost bins, irrigation systems and rows of raised beds filled with soft, black compost" donated by the Bronx Zoo, writes Rachel Wharton in the *New York Daily News*.

What can you do to promote sustainable local industries and a better environment?

I made the earth, and created humankind upon it. (Isaiah 45:12)

Thank You, Lord of the Harvest, for earth's stupendous bounty. Make us its careful stewards.

On Being Happy

Although optimism and a positive attitude can't cure all, science is finding the value in laughter and happiness.

Over time, the editors at *Psychotherapy Networker* magazine have covered studies, which they note were recently brought to the general public by *Time* magazine in a special section entitled "The Science of Happiness."

"The *Time* issue includes several tips for promoting a greater sense of well-being for oneself, such as keeping a gratitude journal, building a social support network, consciously laughing (even if your heart's not in it), focusing on whatever you're doing, and practicing acts of kindness and altruism."

Time's primer on positive psychology looked at "the connections between optimism and health and between religion and well-being, the neurobiology of happiness, the beneficial effects of laughter, the false allure of money and materialism."

Seek your happiness in the simple moments of everyday living—and your relationship with God.

A glad heart makes a cheerful countenance. (Proverbs 15:13)

It's not always easy to be cheerful, Jesus. Help me to concentrate on the positive.

Anonymous No More

Have you ever read a piece of literature attributed only to Anonymous and wondered about the author?

You may be familiar with "Desiderata," which was popular in the 1950's and '60's. Because it was copied and shared, without author credit, by a church founded in 1692, that date stuck, and readers presumed it was a old piece of wisdom, rediscovered.

In fact, Max Ehrmann, a writer from Indiana, wrote the poem in 1927. It was published in 1948, three years after his death. In time, the mystery was solved and the author got credit for his work. Here is an excerpt:

"Go placidly amid the noise and haste, and remember what peace there may be in silence.

"And whatever your labors and aspirations, in the noisy confusion of life, keep peace in your soul. With all its sham, drudgery and broken dreams, it is still a beautiful world. Be cheerful. Strive to be happy."

The rich, and the eminent, and the poor—their glory is the fear of the Lord. (Sirach 10:22)

Holy Creator, remind me that I am here because You want me to be here.

Walking–and Acting–in Good Faith

Since age six, Tim Carey has been part of the Walk to Cure Diabetes. Carey, who was diagnosed with the disease when he was four years old, has raised more than $50,000 in a dozen years.

But this Albany teen doesn't limit his acts of kindness to a once-a-year event. Year-round, he visits shut-in parishioners of Albany's St. James Catholic Church as well as residents of a neighborhood nursing home.

"They are extraordinarily happy to talk to someone," Carey explains of these visits to the sick and the elderly. "You're bringing them a lot of happiness–and the look on their faces makes you glad you went."

All his actions are motivated by his faith, Carey says. "It's a constant," he explains.

For all of us, in good times and bad, it helps to have the constancy of God's love to lean on.

You are precious in My sight, and honored, and I love you. ...Do not fear, for I am with you. (Isaiah 43:4,5)

Father, when I grow weary, fretful or fearful today, walk with me, offering me Your calmness, hope and love.

Family Time

Michele Hirshman, her husband and their two sons gather at 9 p.m. for Torah study four days a week.

Married to a law school professor, she says, "It's very bad not to show up (at school) when your kid is expecting you!" So she makes an effort to be there for them.

When Michele Hirshman is not caring for her family, she works as first deputy to Eliot Spitzer, New York State's attorney general. The lawyer has a distinguished background: she earned a B.A. summa cum laude with highest department honors in the history of Rutgers College, graduated from Yale Law School and spent several years as a high-level federal prosecutor. Her current duties make her, the "gatekeeper, teacher and moral and legal authority" for 600 lawyers in 15 offices.

Michele Hirshman is one of many women who are professionals, wives and mothers. Encourage them and all busy people to find a holy balance in their lives.

Take care that you do not forget the Lord. (Deuteronomy 6:12)

God, inspire women and men to balance their responsibilities so that there is always time for You.

A Fishy Story

Eric Bartos was so distraught over the break-up of his marriage that, while fishing with friends, he took off his wedding band and slipped it over the bill of a sailfish he'd just caught. He released the fish, allowing it to swim off with the ring.

Bartos and his friends never discussed the incident again, until Bartos caught the same sailfish two years later, the ring still around its bill.

As unlikely as the story may seem, Bartos' friends had photos of both events, and Bartos passed a polygraph exam paid for by a local radio station.

Bartos' ex-wife never questioned the story.

"I believed it from the start," she said. "Maybe this is a sign [for us]...to make peace."

Incredible twists of fate aren't necessary for us to reach out to those from whom we may be estranged. Do you have anyone with whom it may be time to make peace?

Blessed are the peacemakers for they will be called children of God. (Matthew 5:9)

Lord, help me to be fair, to forgive and to accept forgiveness.

All in an Honest Day's Work

New York City subway motorman Aloysis Herman didn't think it was anything unusual when he saw a black bag in an empty subway car at the end of his shift.

But when Herman discovered more than $18,000 in cash and checks in the bag, he was stunned. "I never saw that kind of money before," he says.

Imagine how stunned his co-workers were when Herman turned the bag over to the police. "A lot of them were calling me crazy," he admits.

Herman felt anything but crazy when, after recovering the cash from the police, the woman who had lost the money came to thank him. She told him that she had taken the money out of the bank to pay her son's college tuition. "She told me she was happy that I made it possible for her son to go to college," says Herman.

It takes faith to act honorably. Adhere to your ideals. Your choices define your character.

Honesty comes home to those who practice it. (Sirach 27:9)

Lord Jesus, You taught us how to be strong in the face of adversity. Help me hang on to my faith in difficult times.

The Priest Who Makes Toys

Monsignor James Hannon's garage in Ocean Springs, Mississippi, is filled with sawdust, lumber, as well as finished and unfinished toys.

Born in County Galway, Ireland, this 85-year-old Catholic priest has been the energy behind a wooden toy ministry for the past two decades. In fact, every year in December, he dons his red hat and distributes his handmade toys to underprivileged children throughout the area.

Using mostly donated wood to make 60 to 70 toys per year, he got his interest in woodworking from his father Patrick, who built the family's living room table.

Now retired, the man known as Father Christmas to locals also volunteers at a free pharmacy in Biloxi, celebrates daily Mass at the Villa Maria retirement home, and fills in for vacationing area priests.

No matter the work we do, it is blessed if done in a spirit of love.

Let the favor of the Lord our God be upon us, and prosper for us the work of our hands. (Psalm 90:17)

Bless the work of our hands, Father. May all we do give You praise.

Tropical Medicines in the Making

When Carolann Sharkey's beloved husband was diagnosed with a brain tumor, the couple tried everything, including medicinal plants, to cure him.

After he died, Sharkey, still curious about the potential tropical plants held to effect cures, moved to Key West to start a new life.

While attending a conference on native plants, she approached the keynote speaker and said simply, "We need your help." The two collaborated, and their efforts resulted in the Key West Tropical Forest and Botanical Garden, which nurtures rare Caribbean and Florida Keys plants and supports research on the plants' medicinal qualities.

Asking for help demonstrates both courage and wisdom. No one is an island. Much can be accomplished when we work together.

The Lord created medicines out of the earth. (Sirach 38:4)

Lord Jesus, may I never become too "big" to ask for help from others.

Talking about Prayer

People who pray have lots of company. According to *The New York Times,* eight out of ten Americans say they pray every day, or at least weekly. Only nine percent say they never pray.

According to a *Christian Science Monitor* survey, people pray for guidance (62%); to give thanks or praise (54%); to be forgiven (47%). Some also pray for health and healing; good weather; or some sort of victory.

Yet not everyone agrees that prayer should be the subject of research. Some scientists are angry when government money funds such studies. Some religious people feel scientific research cheapens religion. Some people are even "mystified that anyone would be presumptuous enough to entreat God for favors."

While many do make particular requests of God, adoration, thanksgiving and repentance also play a large role in the spirituality of many. However you pray, strive to stay mindful of God's presence in your life.

"Pray then in this way: Our Father..."
(Matthew 6:9)

Jesus, teach me to pray as You would have me pray.

Rock On...'Til Bedtime

Rock music has typically been seen as an entertainment of the young. Some musicians, however, have been blurring the line as to just how young: Bands like They Might Be Giants have used their success with older audiences to transition into the world of children's music.

They Might Be Giants, whose biggest audiences can usually be found on college campuses, have already recorded two albums for kindergarten-age youngsters. These albums include kid-friendly tracks like "Alphabet of Nations," which features the lyric, "Algeria! Bulgaria! Cambodia! Dominica!"

John Flansburgh, a member of the band, says that writing songs for children isn't much of a stretch. Two things are necessary: Make the song entertaining, and don't talk down to the kids.

Each of us has talents and abilities we can apply in countless, unexpected ways. How can you use your gifts in a new way?

A man...summoned his slaves and entrusted his property to them; to one he gave five talents, to another two, to another one, to each according to his ability. (Matthew 25:14-15)

Lord, help me to expand my horizons.

Caring for All God's Creatures

"I don't care where you live, Beverly Hills or Skid Row, if you love your dog, the tears are the same."

Cited as one of *Family Circle* magazine's Women Who Make a Difference, Lori Weisc saw stray dogs scrounging for food in downtown Los Angeles and decided to act. She fed them and took them to a vet, but soon realized this was just the tip of the iceberg. There were hundreds of needy dogs on the streets, many of them companions to homeless people.

Along with a co-worker, Richard Tuttlemondo, Weisc founded Downtown Dog Rescue. They've rescued hundreds of starving and abused canines and found them homes. Other dogs are nursed to health but stay with homeless people for whom "the animal is all they have," Weise notes.

Although she started out helping the dogs, Weise has also befriended men and women living on the streets.

Compassion has a ripple effect.

He had compassion for them, because they were harassed and helpless, like sheep without a shepherd. (Matthew 9:36)

Compassionate Jesus, remind us to care not just for our fellow human beings but for all creatures, all creation.

What Do You See?

When Erik Weihenmayer met a group of visually impaired Tibetan teenagers, he saw amazing possibilities for them, even as many of their neighbors saw them as outcasts possessed by demons.

Weihenmayer had heard about the youngsters from Sabriye Tenberken, a blind German expatriate living in Tibet and the founder of Braille Without Borders. Shocked by the adversity they faced, she started a vocational school in 1998 and created a Tibetan Braille language.

Tenberken invited Weihenmayer, the first blind man to climb to the summit of Mount Everest, to speak to her students. He wanted to do more, so he organized a climbing expedition with them through the Himalayans. "These kids haven't been born into all the opportunity I've had. I wanted to be that opportunity for these kids."

The teens climbed farther than they, or others, might ever have expected. How far can others go with your help?

The blind receive their sight, the lame walk, the lepers are cleansed, the deaf hear, the dead are raised, the poor have good news brought to them. (Luke 7:22)

Holy Spirit, we are all blind in some way. Help us to see all You want us to see.

Message in a Bottle

Ever wonder how to get a ship inside a bottle?

The work is tedious and labor-intensive. There are no shortcuts. Says one craftsperson, "I must painstakingly craft each separate piece of the model to the correct scale, and then place them through the neck into the bottle." This is accomplished through thin, metal tongs and hooks to guide each piece into place.

That same model builder admits that "halfway through each ship, there is a time when I'm tempted to send it through the window out of pure frustration." Yet, something motivates him to keep working at his task.

The result is a wondrous, intricate work of art.

What serves as a source of motivation in your life? Think about a time when you found the fortitude to keep going in the face of adversity. In times of adversity, can you be a source of fortitude for another?

Help the afflicted. (1 Timothy 5:10)

Jesus, You know how frustrating life can be. Walk with me so that I don't become discouraged. Help me stay my course.

Legendary Expertise, Hidden in Paris

His curious little shop is hardly noticeable to those rushing by. But its obscurity belies its individuality, gentle elegance, and place in music history. Andre Bissonnet's quaint and picturesque shop, Instruments Musicaux Anciens, contains an eclectic collection of musical instruments dating from the 15th century.

The collection includes a porcelain violin with exquisite floral patterns, an unorthodox twisted trumpet in perfect working order and antique mandolins, lutes, banjos, violins and other rare and unique musical instruments collected over the decades.

Today, Bissonnet's expertise is legendary, his counsel sought worldwide.

Deceptive appearances cause us to underestimate the worth of a person. Giving others the benefit of the doubt is the wisest choice.

Do not judge by appearances but judge with right judgment. (John 7:24)

Jesus, each and every person I meet is precious and valuable in Your eyes. Help me treat them as such.

Lighting Candles for Kindness

"Kindness is the truest religion," says 76-year-old Alice Johnson. "Kindness is love in action."

Johnson decided to make that message known through a series of books written by south Florida public school children. They tell how the kindness of family and friends has touched their lives.

"They are stories that touch lives and lift spirits," explains Johnson, a retired educator. The idea of having children write about kindness came to her after September 11, 2001, when she heard the terrorists described as very religious people. "Yet they were so unkind," Johnson observes.

Johnson said her *Candlelight* series of books serves as a monument to what happened on that tragic day. "Kindness encompasses all of the virtues," Johnson explains. "In kindness you find forgiveness and patience and understanding and self-control."

Bring kindness to your world today.

Show kindness and mercy to one another. (Zechariah 7:9)

Kind and merciful Father, hear our prayers for peace with justice.

The Little Plane that Did

It may not have flown high or swiftly, but it flew—over the Atlantic Ocean, no less.

Maynard Hill's 11-pound, six-foot long balsa wood and mylar plane made the trip from Canada to Ireland with a few drops of fuel to spare, according to witnesses. The flight, guided by remote controls and enthusiastic supporters, took roughly 39 hours.

"A great cheer went up when we saw it land," says Dave Brown, who handled the controls for the landing. "It was so thrilling."

Nothing is accomplished without one individual believing, in his or her heart, that anything is possible. Try and remove the limits binding your own imagination and spirit—and see what you can accomplish!

Hope does not disappoint us. (Romans 5:5)

An optimistic heart is Your gift, Lord. Thank You for all people and things that inspire me to keep a positive outlook.

With God on Our Side

Psychologist Carl Jung once said that a great deal of institutional religion seemed designed to prevent people from having a spiritual experience. Clearly, religious differences have spawned wars and discrimination throughout history.

Religious scholar Karen Armstrong believes there is a simple answer: the world's spiritual and religious leaders need to teach and practice compassion. This is the foundation of Jesus' message and ministry, as well the essence of most religious teachings around the world.

Armstrong reminds us that the word compassion does not mean to feel sorry for, but rather, to feel with someone. Compassion entails entering another's point of view and recognizing the similarities that unite you. And she believes that if more of the world's religious leaders stressed compassion we might see less violence "in the name of God."

How can you practice compassion today?

The Lord has compassion for...He knows how we were made...that we are dust.
(Psalm 103:13,14)

Father, may the world's religious leaders—as well as all believers—find common ground and unity.

It's How You Play the Game

It's been said that in sports, "It isn't whether you win or lose, it's how you play the game." This adage seems especially true when one considers safety.

Even under the best of circumstances, no sports activity is risk-free. However, by taking precautions, most serious hazards are preventable. Before engaging in (or allowing children to participate in) sports, consider the following tips:

- Wear a helmet, eye guards, masks and other protective equipment to reduce the likelihood and severity of injuries.
- Warm up thoroughly.
- Don't overtrain. Watch out for heatstroke.
- Have a thorough medical exam before participating, particularly in strenuous activity.
- Have a clear emergency plan and a first-aid kit on hand.

Sports and exercise should be healthy activities. Take care of yourself and others to be sure your participation is good for your mind and body.

In His image, in the image of God He created them. (Genesis 1:27)

God, my body and mind are Your gifts to me. Help me keep them safe and healthy.

Credit for a Life

Two women met on a cross-country trip. They were the only young people on the bus, so they bonded instantly. At the end of their journey, they vowed to keep in touch.

They did. Over the following decades, they faithfully traded letters. Sixty-two years later, they decided to meet again.

They spent a weekend together, still fast friends. At the end of their good-bye dinner, one asked the other a question: If they had to live their lives again, exactly as they were, would they do it? One said yes, the other said no.

"What does that signify?" asked the satisfied one.

"That you liked your life," answered the other.

"Maybe," the satisfied woman conceded. "And maybe that you don't give yourself credit for yours."

We can't change all the circumstances of our lives, but we can change how we view them. Give yourself credit for your life.

Take delight in the Lord...Commit your way to the Lord; trust in Him. (Psalm 37:5)

Lord, help me to see the good in my life and my actions.

Finding Time

Admittedly, there never seems to be enough time for all that you have to do, let alone for what you would like to do. And what about making time for God and developing your spirituality?

August Gold of the Sacred Center for Spiritual Living in New York City makes these suggestions for nurturing your spirit with the time you have:

- Commit yourself to the time before your first cup of coffee, before your day has begun—while others are still sleeping
- Read an inspirational text for five minutes
- Write in a journal for five minutes
- Sit, meditating or praying for five minutes
- Take deep breaths to align body, mind and heart during the day

Our dear God is a patient lover who waits—and wants—to hear from us. Let's communicate with God everyday.

> **Daniel (got)...down on his knees three times a day to pray to his God and to praise Him. (Daniel 6:10)**

> *God, enable me to make time for us—You and me.*

Building Justice

There are two sides to Nancy Jochens. By day, the Kansas City, Missouri, lawyer works in commercial bankruptcy and creditor's rights litigation. In her spare time, she helps to build houses and communities for the El Salvadoran poor through Homes from the Heart, an organization she co-founded.

"I have a genuine desire for justice, and I believe in charity," Jochens explains. "Charity is sharing your bounty with others. Justice is helping people get what should already be theirs—their God-given rights as human beings."

She also sells coffee grown and harvested on small El Salvadoran farms, with the proceeds going to those still homeless after the 2001 earthquakes.

"There's so much more to do," Jochens says. And she plans to stick with it.

Each of us is called to make a difference in addition to making a living. How will you do that?

Help the poor for the commandment's sake. (Sirach 29:9)

Merciful Father, show me how to make a living and a difference.

Laugh It Up

Of course, it feels good to laugh. But, more than that, laughter is good for us.

Dr. Clifford Kuhn, professor of psychiatry at the University of Louisville School of Medicine, says, "If medicine could harness the proven health benefits of laughter, drug companies would be knocking themselves out to get the patent."

According to Dr. Kuhn, author of *The Fun Factor*, scientists who have studied the subject have concluded that laughter: reduces the level of stress hormones, perks up the immune system, relaxes muscles, clears the respiratory tract, increases circulation and eases perceived pain.

Researcher Lee Berk of California's Loma Linda University adds that because laughter both stimulates and soothes us, we feel "enlivened, refreshed and clear-headed, much as we do after an aerobic workout."

Every day brings its share of problems. Make sure it brings laughter, as well. For your own sake and for those around you: laugh it up!

Our mouth was filled with laughter, and our tongue with shouts of joy. (Psalm 126:2)

Spirit of Joy, help me to rejoice in Your many gifts, including delight in good humor and healthy laughter.

Appreciating the Beauty of Poetry

For many, poetry is a most beautiful way–even the best way–to express how they feel. It can be a solitary appreciation, but doesn't have to be.

Since 1985 Poets House in New York City has been a place where poetry lovers and learners gather to share, read, write and enjoy poetry. Founded by former U.S. poet laureate Stanley Kunitz and arts administrator Elizabeth Kray, it is a place to elevate the spirit.

"There was a sense that poets were terribly lonely in our culture and they needed a place to gather and meet each other," said Lee Briccetti, executive director.

Over the years, Poets House has grown to its current $1 million annual budget, which comes from public funds, foundations, corporations and individual donors.

Says Briccetti, "If God is in the details, Poets House is poetry heaven."

Commit your work to the Lord. (Proverbs 16:3)

God, inspire poets and writers, indeed all communicators.

Clothing with a Conscience

Like many celebrities, Bono, lead singer of the rock band U2, has ventured into the world of fashion by acting as spokesperson for a clothing line. Unlike many, however, Bono is using his new venture to do good.

Edun, a clothing line co-designed by Bono's wife, Ali Hewson, and Rogan Gregory, a designer known for emphasizing ethical guidelines, has a unique way of doing business. Edun studies the manufacturing capabilities of poor nations, and then designs clothing based on what will make the most of local resources and talents.

The end result is not only fashionable clothing, but new jobs and stable commercial ties in countries like Peru, Tunisia, South Africa and Tanzania.

Profit and philanthropy are not necessarily mutually exclusive. A sense of conscience and responsibility, partnered with a drive to succeed, can be a powerful combination.

Give and it will be given to you. ...The measure you give will be the measure you get back. (Luke 6:38)

Lord, help me always to remember that I have responsibilities toward all the world.

More Than Make-Believe

What many of us refer to as "child's play," as it turns out, may actually be a form of adulthood "training."

According to a professor of psychology at Sarah Lawrence College, when youngsters play, pretend and use their imaginations, they are cultivating the skills necessary to grow into smart, adaptive adults.

Pretending and playing "make-believe," say experts, helps sharpen kids' minds, develop flexibility; and it keeps them open to new opportunities. What's more, games that include role-playing ("Let's play house!") can foster a greater fluency in language, spatial orientation and even academic readiness.

Children need the gift of time and space to play. Says one expert, "There's nothing like the power of pretend."

The streets of the city shall be full of boys and girls playing in its streets. (Zechariah 8:5)

Jesus, may we imitate Your love, compassion and respect for children and the child-like.

Unexpected Finds

As paleontologists were attempting to transport fossils excavated at Montana's Hell Creek Formation, they encountered a problem: the only way to transport the fossilized dinosaur bones was on a helicopter, yet one, a thighbone from a Tyrannosaurus rex, wouldn't fit.

Reluctantly, the researchers broke the bone to put it in the helicopter. The disappointment they felt, however, was soon overshadowed by the enormity of what they found: The bone contained soft tissue, the first ever recovered from a dinosaur.

Similar material was soon found in other bones, requiring a revisualization of science's understanding of fossilization. Such finds will also allow scientists to study dinosaur physiology in ways never before possible.

What had begun as a misfortune turned into a magnificent opportunity to increase humanity's knowledge. Keep an open mind, even in disappointment. Great opportunities may await you.

Hope for good things. (Sirach 2:9)

Lord, help me always to find the good, even in disappointment.

Overnight Success?

Not every successful person does well right from the start of their careers. Take, for example, Margo Robinson.

She had had a difficult personal life and yearned for meaningful work, but had a hard time finding it. One day, she applied for a job at a mortgage bank, even though she lacked experience. When a winter storm kept other candidates from the interview, she got there–and got the position. Within months, Robinson had secured $1 million in accounts.

A few years later, she started her own mortgage brokerage firm. She's now so respected in her field that she shares her experience on a radio show. "Every single thing that took place in my life happened for a purpose and led me to be who I am," says Margo Robinson. "We can't go back and change things, but we always have the ability to create something new."

Choose to create something new, something good, today.

Let us choose what is right. (Job 34:4)

Holy Spirit, it's so easy to get discouraged. During difficult times keep hope alive within me.

You Say "Great," I Say "Hunky Dory"

It seems every generation has its own lexicon. Words come and go, like fashion, and in time, one's generational slang becomes unrecognizable "ancient history" to another.

Nevertheless, it can be fun to reminisce. Do any of these words or phrases *ring a bell*?

The bee's knees

The cat's meow

Nifty

Neat

Groovy (a cousin to "far out!")

Swell

I'll be a monkey's uncle!

While it's hard to hear the language of our youth go out of style, author Richard Lederer says that is merely natural change. He says, "We...have been blessed to live in changeful times."

What a beautiful way to perceive change! After all, change is inevitable, but the way we deal with it isn't.

I the Lord do not change. (Malachi 3:6)

Abba, change can be unsettling and scary, or exhilarating and rejuvenating. Help me cope with change.

Telling Yourself to Get Lost—and Liking It

As host of the television series, *The Amazing Race,* Phil Keoghan has mastered the art of finding his way around the planet.

In his own life, however, he relishes tossing away the map and deliberately getting lost. Keoghan contends that many people have become too caught up in planning, scheduling and trying to control every moment of their lives, thus missing out on the thrill of detouring into the unknown.

"The key is to break your routine, veer off the beaten path—and let yourself wander," he states.

The secret to enjoying a "lost" moment, Keoghan explains, is allowing yourself to relax. But he cautions: "Wherever you go, be sure to 'unplug' from the rest of the world. If everybody knows how to reach you, you're not lost."

In treasuring every moment of life—lost or found—we say a great "Amen!" in thanksgiving for God's great gift of life.

I came that they may have life, and have it abundantly. (John 10:10)

Thanks, Creator, for the gift of every minute of this day.

A Helping of Neighborliness

It wasn't hard to figure out why Julie Dahlberg and her husband, Scott, struggled with the biblical command to "love your neighbor."

"We didn't even know who they were," Julie admits.

To remedy that, Julie and Scott began "Soup Night." Once a week, the Dahlbergs invite their neighbors, sometimes up to 30 families, into their home for soup and fellowship. Guests are asked only to bring bread or salad; or just themselves and a smile. No RSVP is required. "We never know who or how many will show up, but we know it will be an evening of good food and great conversation," says Julie.

How well do you know those who live closest to you? Have you reached out to make new neighbors feel welcome? Laying the foundation of neighborliness can build a lifetime of caring friendships.

**Love your neighbor as yourself.
(Matthew 22:39)**

Bless those who extend a welcoming hand to the newcomer, the displaced, the lonely, the sick or elderly, Father.

Things to Remember

Marshall Field, who founded the department store of the same name, compiled this list of twelve things to remember.

1. –The value of time
2. –The success of perseverance
3. –The pleasure of working
4. –The dignity of simplicity
5. –The worth of character
6. –The power of kindness
7. –The influence of example
8. –The obligation of duty
9. –The wisdom of economy
10. –The virtue of patience
11. –The improvement of talent
12. –The joy of originating

Each of these twelve is worth considering in regard to how we lead–and would like to lead–our lives.

If riches are a desirable possession in life, what is richer than wisdom, the active cause of all things? (Wisdom of Solomon 8:5)

Spirit of Wisdom, instruct me in understanding what is important to You and should be important to me.

Choose to be Faithful

Have you ever wished you could just get away from it all?

There's a tale told of a medieval king who tired of the burdens of being a ruler and the life of the court. He decided to enter a monastery.

However, the abbot warned him, "Your Majesty, do you understand that the vow here is one of obedience? That will be hard because you are used to having power."

The king answered, "I understand. For the rest of my life I will be obedient to you, as Christ leads you."

"Then I will tell you what to do," said the abbot. "Go back to your throne and serve faithfully in the place where God has placed you."

And when the king died, this was inscribed on his tombstone: "The king learned to rule by being obedient."

We may not always understand what God asks of us, but we can still do His will. We can be faithful.

Then I said, "Here I am;...I delight to do Your will, O my God. (Psalm 40:6,7)

Guide me, Precious Lord, in being Your loving child, Your faithful servant, Your hope-filled messenger.

Keeping Up Your Spirit at Work

It's bound to happen. At some point in the work day, the copier will jam, a coworker will get on your nerves, or you'll be unable to find the one piece of paper you need right away.

Here are some steps to help you focus on God "on the job."

Start the day with a prayer. Pray to keep God with you through all the day throws at you.

Keep His picture on your desk. Well not exactly a snapshot in a frame, but some visual reminder of the spiritual.

Do the best job you can—Someone does notice. Being and doing our best—and serving—others is our thanks for the unique gifts and talents God has given us.

Set a time to stop. Don't let work drown out God or family.

We live in God's presence—and nine to five is no exception.

Commit your work to the Lord. (Proverbs 16:3)

Master, as I serve You today, use me to show Your face to someone, to bring them Your love.

Keeping Open the Door to Hope

For years, sisters Hana Katz and Klara Bleier believed that the other had died, like the rest of their family, in the Nazi death camp at Auschwitz, Poland.

Separated in 1944, each sister tried to get on with her life. Ironically, each settled in Israel in 1948 and raised families, 45 miles apart from each other. Yet, neither knew of the other's whereabouts.

It was Klara Bleier's son-in-law, who wanted to fill in the blanks about his wife's family history, who helped bring the two women together. When they were finally reunited after 61 years, the experience was overwhelming. "I suddenly felt faint and couldn't catch my breath," says Hana Katz. "This just shows that God doesn't close all the doors."

Hope truly does spring eternal. Where there's life, there's hope.

> **To (Israelites) belong the adoption, the glory, the covenants, the giving of the law, the worship, and the promises...the patriarchs, and from them...comes the Messiah...God. (Romans 9:4,5)**

Holy Spirit, may I never lose the ability to hope.

Seeds in the Soul

Perhaps more than any other season of the year, spring makes even the most urban among us think about the beauty of nature. We search for the first crocus and the budding of the trees, awakening as winter's icy grip is broken.

It's a good time to contemplate our own spiritual growth.

"Every moment and every event of every person's life on earth plants something in the soul," wrote Thomas Merton, the spiritual writer and Trappist monk.

"For just as the wind carries thousands of winged seeds, so each moment brings with it germs of spiritual vitality that come to rest imperceptibly in the minds and wills of people. Most of these unnumbered seeds perish and are lost, because we are not prepared to receive them: for such seeds as these cannot spring up anywhere except in the good soil of freedom, spontaneity and love."

Nurture the seeds of hope. Encourage them to blossom.

I have put my hope in the Everlasting. (Baruch 4:22)

Generous Creator, thank You for the miracles of life and of eternity.

Everyday Hero

It started out as just an ordinary day for both Kelly Capitani and Ron Gross, but by the time it had ended, their lives had been changed forever.

During her lunch break Capitani was walking in downtown York, Pennsylvania, when she was grabbed and dragged into an alley. Although she screamed, windows and doors shut around her, as witnesses chose to turn away.

Ron Gross chose otherwise. The young attorney and father of two little girls heard her screams, and intervened. When the assailant pulled out a gun, Ron was sure he would be killed. Miraculously, though the thug struck Ron viciously, he then walked away. Ron and Kelly clung to one another, amazed that they were still alive.

Ron Gross exhibited bravery in the face of mortal danger to help a complete stranger. His compassion and selflessness echoed Jesus' words: "Whatsoever you do to the least of my brothers, that you do unto Me."

Do to others as you would have them do to you. (Luke 6:31)

Father God, I pray that in a moment of crisis I will be willing to risk myself for the sake of others.

How to Be Holy

It's not easy to become a saint. But it may be simple.

Catherine de Hueck Doherty, founder of Madonna House in Ontario, believed in doing little things well for the love of God:

"Let every day be the day of beginning again, of loving Him a little more, of hungering for Him a little more, of turning your face to Him...you shall be judged on love alone.

"There is only one way to love God and to prove it to Him, and that is by loving your neighbor– the person next to you at any given moment... turning your face and heart to Christ simply means turning your face to the one who is next to you at this moment in your life. If you do that...you shall become a saint."

Ask God to help you grow in holiness.

I, your Lord and Teacher...have set you an example, that you also should do as I have done to you. (John 13:13, 15)

Jesus, Lord of all saints and sinners, inspire me to love my neighbor and myself always for love of You.

On Serving and Leading

True leadership and service go hand-in-hand. Here is a prayer from a world leader who lives out that concept.

May I become at all times, both now and forever:

A protector for those without protection
A guide for those who have lost their way
A ship for those with oceans to cross
A bridge for those with rivers to cross
A sanctuary for those in danger
A lamp for those without light
A place of refuge for those who lack shelter
And a servant to all in need.

The writer of these words is the 14th Dalai Lama of Tibet. He is not only the spokesperson for his people's non-violent struggle for independence, but a respected advocate for inter-religious understanding and advocate for world peace. In 1989, he won the Nobel Peace Prize.

Give others the best you have–both as leader and servant.

He poured water into a basin and began to wash the disciples feet. (John 13:5)

Beloved Lord of all, guide me on the path of peace, the path to You.

A Twin Surprise

Each year, about 1.4 million high school seniors in the United States take the Scholastic Aptitude Test (SAT). The test is often used by college admissions officers to decide on potential college placement for prospective students. In 2004, only .067% of the SAT-taking students earned a perfect score.

Two of those students were Dillon and Jesse Smith, twin brothers from Long Island, New York. The results are even more confounding when you take into account that neither brother had participated in an SAT review course, an increasingly popular choice for students prepping for the exams. The Smith brothers instead simply studied together and quizzed each other.

Life is full of unexpected surprises, even in the face of the stiffest of odds. Be open to those surprises and enjoy them when they come.

Hope does not disappoint us. (Romans 5:5)

Lord, help me to maintain hope and remind me to be grateful for my blessings.

Mount Morris Counts on Mona

The people of Mount Morris, Pennsylvania, rely on Mona Counts to care for their aches, pains and unusual symptoms.

Many residents of this small Appalachian village earn a modest income, lack health insurance and hesitate to travel to big-city medical centers. Too, they no longer have a full-time local physician.

It was to care for these people that nurse-practitioner Counts opened the Mount Morris Primary Care Center, financed by her and her coal miner husband. Counts, who has a Ph.D. and background as a professor of nursing at Penn State University is sensitive to the community's needs: "They wanted somebody who understood who they were, who didn't talk down to them," she says.

Her patients appreciate her dedication and respond to the respect she gives. "She talked to you like you were another human being, not another dollar," says one patient.

Show respect to all you meet.

Pay respect to whom respect is due. (Romans 13:7)

Remind us, Jesus, that every human being deserves respect.

Where You Want Me to Go

Franciscan Father Mychal Judge loved his life.

A native New Yorker, he loved his hometown and the people he served, especially the firefighters. He was their chaplain. On September 11, 2001, he died along with 342 other members of the fire department and thousands of other people. This is Mychal Judge's prayer, which he said every day:

Lord, take me where You want me to go,

Let me meet who You want me to meet,

Tell me what You want me to say

And keep me out of Your way.

The day before his death, Father Judge spoke at the dedication of a firehouse. He said, "We can never thank God enough for the reality of the lives we have. ...You do what God has called you to do. You show up, you put one foot in front of another...you have no idea what God's calling you to, but He needs you."

Go where God wants you to go.

May (I) gain Christ and be found in Him, not having a righteousness of my own that comes from the law, but one that comes through faith in Christ. (Philippians 3:8-9)

You need me to do something with my life that no one else can do, Holy God. Help me do it.

Dream On

Most of us have a hard time enduring pain for a few minutes, never mind several hours. Imagine being in pain every minute of every day of your life?

Berendina Maazel's rheumatoid arthritis, which has plagued her for over 60 years, has not permitted her any respite from agonizing pain.

Chronic pain has not, however, prevented Maazel from living her life. She has never given up on her dreams, including marriage, travel and painting beautiful images of nature.

"They all came true," she says of her dreams. When asked how she endures in the face of constant pain, her answer is simple: "By hanging onto my dreams!"

Everyone needs to dream because dreams fortify and invigorate the soul, offering insight into who we really are.

(Jacob) dreamed that there was a ladder...to heaven; and the angels of God were ascending and descending on it. And the Lord stood beside him and said..."I will not leave you until I have done what I have promised you." (Genesis 28:12-13,15)

Holy Spirit, help me hold fast to Your dreams for me.

Small Steps to Save the Planet

Don't let the world's pollution problems overwhelm you.

Think small. *The Guardian* newspaper listed 50 suggestions to make a positive difference. Here are several:

- Wrap gifts in fabric and tie with ribbon; both are reusable.
- Start a compost heap.
- Slow down; your car will use less fuel. Carpool. Ride a bike when you can.
- Take quick showers, not baths, to save water.
- Choose energy efficient appliances.
- Use a mug at the office, not polystyrene cups.
- Clean the coils in back of your refrigerator.

Think "green." We'll breathe easier tomorrow knowing we're preserving our beautiful Earth for future generations.

The Lord...formed the earth...He did not create it a chaos, He formed it to be inhabited! (Isaiah 45:18)

Creator, inspire our smallest effort to preserve what's left of Earth's loveliness.

Dealing with Doubt

If you have ever been troubled by doubt, you're not alone.

And if there's one person that's synonymous with doubt, it's St. Thomas the Apostle. He refused to believe the disciples who said they had seen Jesus, risen from the dead. When Jesus appeared to Thomas and the others a week later, He said, "Peace be with you....Have you believed because you have seen Me? Blessed are those who have not seen and yet have come to believe." (John 20:26,29)

Many people have doubts at times. That can be frightening. God wants us to believe, just as He wants us to hope and love. But God understands us better than we do ourselves. After all, God created us with reason and free will. He expects us to use our minds as well as our hearts. Never be afraid to think about God.

Peace be with you!

(Thomas) said to them, "Unless I see the mark of the nails in His hands, and put my finger in the mark of the nails and my hand in His side, I will not believe." (John 20:25)

Prince of Peace, help us turn to You when we are troubled by doubts and fears.

Catering Change

Four years ago, Linda Watson, a single mother of four children and a recovering drug addict, was living in a shelter in Washington, D.C. "My life was not going right," she says, "and I wanted to turn it around."

Watson enrolled in a 12-week culinary program at DC Central Kitchen, which helps train and employ homeless people in the culinary arts. Graduating at the top of her class, she worked her way up to banquet chef at the Grand Hyatt Hotel.

Recently, she has returned to help others at DC Central Kitchen by being a sous-chef at its affiliate, Fresh Start, a catering company that gives its proceeds back to the Kitchen's charitable programs.

Watson says her eldest son, also a recovering addict, has told her: "Mom, look at you! You did it—so can I!"

The greatest leaders are often those whose lives inspire, encourage and reflect positive change.

Cast your burden on the Lord and He will sustain you. (Psalm 55:22)

Strengthen me, Lord, when I grow weary from the tests and trials of life.

No Need to Wait

Twenty percent of Americans are chronic procrastinators. This means that twenty percent of the population also feels the effects of procrastination: increased stress, ill health, insomnia and guilt, to name a few.

What can you do to stop the urge to put things off? According to Dr. Gail Saltz, procrastinators should start with these three strategies:

Prioritize. Make a "to do" list with the most important items at the top, and work your way down.

Control your impulses. Many procrastinators jump from task to task. Choose something to do, and then do it until it's done.

Give yourself time. You can't change habits overnight. Take inspiration from the progress you *do* make, and go from there.

Change can only occur if you let it. Give yourself a chance, and you'll be amazed by what happens.

The kingdom of God has come near; repent, and believe in the good news. (Mark 1:15)

Beloved God, help me to see the ways in which I can make my life better.

Pipe Surgeons

A senior manager at a manufacturing company had a problem, albeit a good one: Why was the pipe maintenance group at his plant doing so well?

The work was extremely dirty and repetitive, and the pressure on the crew to keep the expensive machinery operating was tremendous. Why then did this crew have great attendance, almost no turnover and outstanding results?

A consultant he hired found the answer as soon as he entered the plant. The entire crew wore surgical smocks like those doctors wear. The foreman said he'd obtained them from his son, a heart surgeon.

"You wear them for comfort?" asked the consultant.

"No," said the foreman. "It's because we are surgeons." He brought out the crew's mission statement: "To take care of these pipes the way a doctor takes care of your heart."

Every job we do, no matter how small, requires a similar wholehearted effort.

Prosper the work of our hands! (Ps. 90:17)

Jesus of Nazareth, I give You the work of my hands this day. Bless it and keep me safe.

Seeking Cures, Resisting Ignorance

AIDS, cancers and diabetes are familiar diseases. But few in the developed world know about pellagra anymore, though it still occurs in areas of Africa and India.

After the Civil War this disfiguring and debilitating niacin deficiency affected poor rural Southerners whose subsisted on corn meal, molasses and pork fat. Pellagra was said to be transmissible. Patients were quarantined. Cures ranged from arsenic to electroshock.

In 1914, Dr. Joseph Goldberger of the U. S. Public Health Service and Marine Hospital, was assigned to find pellagra's cause and cure while calming the hysteria about it.

Despite ignorance, fear, resistance and derision, Dr. Goldberger found that pellagra was caused by an absence of fresh vegetables, milk and fresh meat in the diets.

Resist ignorance and fear; encourage doctors and scientists to seek the truth for the good of all God's children.

Physician(s)...pray to the Lord that He grant them success in diagnosis and in healing, for the sake of preserving life. (Sirach 38:12,14)

Holy Spirit, inspire researchers who look for the causes and cures of AIDS/HIV, cancer and other diseases.

Your Child's Best–and Imaginary–Friend

If your young child is nurturing a close friendship and the "friend" happens to be imaginary, experts say there's nothing to become alarmed about.

First, such creations are common. Nearly 65% of children up to age seven played with at least one imaginary friend at some point in their lives, according to a study published in *Developmental Psychology* magazine.

What's more, such exercises in imagination give a child a developmental advantage. Experts believe that children who play with imaginary playmates may have an edge in terms of verbal skills, and may develop a superior ability to understand other points of view.

Imagination is a precious and beautiful thing. Find ways to nurture a child's imagination, and you may be helping a child do more than play games.

Let the little children come to Me...for it is to such as these that the kingdom of heaven belongs. (Matthew 19:14)

Bless all little children, Father. Preserve their innocence and optimism in a challenging world.

A Model Program

Everyone knows that fashion models can't be very smart, right?

That's what a Slovenian television program was trying to prove when it subjected a former Miss Universe to a series of tests that assessed her abilities in regard to spatial awareness, mathematical equations and problem solving.

The catch, though, was that the test showed the model, who had dropped out of school at the age of 16, had an IQ of 156–a certifiable genius. In fact, she scored higher than the nuclear physicist the program had recruited to compete against her!

The program, by the way, was soon scrapped. Producers now hope to develop a show searching for the world's smartest model.

Stereotypes restrict the way we see those around us, leading us to short-sightedness and injustice. Have respect for everyone, and let people stand on their own merits.

Pay all of them their dues...respect to whom respect is due, honor to whom honor is due. (Romans 13:7)

Lord, help me to always see the worth of others.

School Supplier

The current school year is not yet over, and Mavis Theodore is already busy working to be sure that homeless Brooklyn students have next year's supplies.

Theodore has organized a fund raising drive to buy pencils, notebooks and other school supplies for kids who live in ten of the county's homeless shelters. "The need is great," she explains. "These children have no other way of getting school supplies."

An administrator of a New Jersey publishing company, Theodore has the support of individuals and local businesses. One year, she and her team of volunteers raised enough money for 600 packages of school supplies. Theodore feels certain they'll eventually make their goal, school supply packages for all the children in the shelters.

Our "neighbor" may not have a home–but we need to have a heart and lend a helping hand.

Love your neighbor as yourself. (Matthew 19:19)

Master, teach us Your ways, so that we may serve You in others.

Two Things Worth Their Salt

Research has shown that ancient Mayan entrepreneurs along the Belize coast constructed massive saltworks and complex trade systems with other Mayans living further inland.

The salt harvesters extracted salt from seawater by boiling it in large ceramic pots. They then paddled it inland in canoes, and traded in large cities, bringing figurines, whistles, pottery and other artifacts back to the coast.

Researchers at Louisiana State University, which led the study that discovered the saltworks, also say that there is no evidence of state support on the part of any Mayan governments. All those involved in the saltworks seem to have been individuals who set up their businesses, trade and transportation themselves, traveling great distances to do so.

Now, as then, ingenuity and hard work go a long way, no matter what the circumstances. How can they help your life?

Do not hate hard labor or farm work, which was created by the Most High. (Sirach 7:15)

Lord, help me to think innovatively and act with motivation.

Children's Definitions of Love

Professionals asked 4 to 8 years olds, "What does love mean?"

Rebecca said that when her grandmother's arthritic hands prevented her from painting her toenails her grandfather did "it for her...even when his hands got arthritis."

"Love is when Mommy sees Daddy smelly and sweaty and still says he is handsomer than Robert Redford," according to Chris.

And according to Cindy, "during my piano recital, I was on stage and I was scared. I...saw my daddy waving and smiling. ...I wasn't scared anymore."

Billy noticed that "When someone loves you, the way they say your name is different. You just know that your name is safe in their mouth."

How do you define love? How do you live love?

Love is patient...kind...not envious or boastful or arrogant or rude...not irritable or resentful...(love) rejoices in the truth. (1 Corinthians 13:4,5,6)

God, make us whole-souled lovers!

Appreciating Native American Contributions

"It's an uplifting feeling for our people to know that we are not alone," said Lance Gumbs, of the Shinnecock Nation at the opening of the National Museum of the American Indian in 2004.

The museum, located on the National Mall in Washington, DC, celebrates the Native Peoples of the Americas in all their vibrancy and variety.

One point made in this "living museum" is that Native Americans from Peru to Alaska aren't relics of the past; they're very much alive despite repeated historic attempts to eliminate them and their cultures.

"I would like anybody who comes to the National Museum of the American Indian to appreciate that native peoples exist through time from a deep and culturally distinctive past right up to the present and into the future," said the museum's first director, W. Richard West, himself descended from a Cheyenne chief.

We owe it to our Creator to appreciate each other.

Without knowledge there is not wisdom. (Sirach 3:25)

Enable us, Holy Spirit, to appreciate each and all of the peoples of the earth.

Saying Thanks

A man, looking like he might be a panhandler, entered a New York City subway car and shouted: "Thank you, ladies and gentlemen!"

"I am not here today to ask you for money. I am here to thank you for what you have already been kind enough to give me over the past few months.

"Your money has allowed me to get these special glasses...I am still legally blind, but now I can read (and) get a job."

When he heard those unexpected words of thanks, one City subway rider was moved to write a letter to the *New York Times* telling the story of one's man's gratitude.

How often have you been approached by a stranger asking for spare change or some food or anything at all? And then there are our friends and family who need a loan or other help.

People give out of the goodness of their hearts, but still they would like to hear words of thanks and appreciation.

Give thanks in all circumstances.
(1 Thessalonians 5:18)

Remind us to express gratitude to each other for the smallest kindness, Merciful Father.

The Point of Practice

Practice makes perfect.

We all know that maxim, but the fact is that it's true. We will never hone any skill unless we work at it. That applies to our talents in such areas as art and writing as well as athletic or performing abilities.

More than that, it takes practice to get good at doing good. The best intentions in the world can't amount to much without applying them everyday.

An elderly woman in a nursing home knows all about that. When a guest visited, she graciously offered coffee and then carefully poured it, even though her movements were slow and a bit unsteady. The woman said, "My mother used to tell me to look each day for something I could do for another to make that person's day a little easier. I've done it every day of my life."

If we don't practice kindness, it may not matter what else we practice.

Clothe yourselves with compassion, kindness, humility, meekness, and patience. (Colossians 3:12)

Jesus, help us imitate You in doing good for all we meet.

Nun on the Run

Sister Janet Fischer is always on the go.

At a rural mission parish in southern Georgia, she stays busy with religious education and community outreach – and as a "foster mom" to area dogs in need of a home.

Since 2002, Sister Janet has made the parish church available for meetings of the Evans County Humane society.

"Having dogs around add a lot to the parish," she says. And she practices what she preaches, giving her home over to four canine guests – Jetter, Tigger, Speckles and Josh.

Feeling the call to religious life in her late teens, Sister Janet recalls, "I didn't really want to go, but God kept pestering me."

And the people in this part of Georgia – and their pets – are glad she listened to God.

Always serve in a spirit of love.

Love the Lord, all you His saints! (Psalm 31:23)

Keep my heart pure, Eternal Father, that I may always love as You do.

Giving Them Hell on Wheels

Kim Adams and her husband Mark first moved to their Piedmont, Oregon, neighborhood in 1987. Living right across the street from Peninsula Park, they saw drug activity, prostitution, and occasional shootings.

"The people in the neighborhood just locked their doors and shut everything, and nobody did anything about it–until we moved here," says Kim Adams.

She leads the Piedmont Foot Patrol which has helped with the crime problem and also with graffiti and street cleanup. Members of the Piedmont Foot Patrol even sit with people waiting for the bus. Disabled by a fall from a galloping horse a year after starting on patrol, Kim first thought she'd quit. But then she got a wheelchair, followed by a motorized scooter to do her duty.

Together, Kim and her volunteers have turned a crime-ridden area into a stable community.

Every change for the better starts with one single step in the right direction.

The Lord is my shepherd. (Psalm 23:1)

Lord, offer all of us Your peace and protection.

Unlikely Partners

What do American sports fishermen have in common with Mongolian Buddhist monks? Both are working to protect the taimen, the world's largest member of the salmon family.

The rare taimen, which can grow to 200 pounds, lives in Mongolia's pristine rivers and streams. It is a favorite of sports fishermen, who practice catch-and-release fishing. But taimen are in danger of disappearing as they have increasingly become a local culinary favorite, and a target for poachers.

That's where the fishermen and monks have joined forces. The fishermen have funded a taimen conservation fund. And they have helped restore a local monastery destroyed almost 70 years ago. In return, the monks use their moral influence to urge people to combat poachers and preserve Mongolia's environment.

Look for creative solutions to problems. And, don't underestimate the help "unlikely partners" may offer.

It is required of stewards that they be found trustworthy. (1 Corinthians 4:2)

Eternal God, help me understand that I am part of nature, and have a responsibility to conserve its wonder.

Seeing Is Believing

Before Cincinnati native and high-school student John Rezanka traveled to Honduras as a volunteer, he had read about the country and its poverty. But, on his arrival, Rezanka said, "I don't think anything you read about or study in school prepares you for what you see here."

John Rezanka was referring to the poverty he encountered in Tegucigalpa. "You hear about how poor people are here...But until you see it, you cannot really understand it," he admits.

Experiencing poverty is a far cry from reading about it. Such an eye-opening experience may remind one, as St. Elizabeth Bayley Seton said, to "live simply so that others can simply live."

What inspires you to help the needy?

Lend to your neighbor in his time of need. (Sirach 29:2)

Father, bless those who give of their time, money and lives to help alleviate others' poverty.

Resorting to Nature

Why resort to nature? Because enjoying Nature – earth, sky, weather, water, plants, trees, animals and birds – is healing.

Employees with window views of nature had less job stress and better overall well-being.

Breast cancer patients who watched birds or walked in a park for half-an-hour three times a week had better quality of life ratings.

Symptoms of attention deficit hyperactivity disorder (ADHD) were reduced after children had enjoyed afternoon or weekend time outdoors.

A study by Deakin University in Australia, found that "parks are a fundamental health resource, particularly in terms of disease prevention." Blood pressure, stress levels and cholesterol decreased; outlook on life increased.

Go for a walk. Watch a bird's flight. Enjoy a sunrise or sunset. Delight in a dog or a squirrel's antics. Relish nature.

O Lord, how manifold are Your works! In wisdom You have made them all. (Psalm 104:24)

Help us, Divine Physician, to find delight and healing in the works of Your hands.

Leaders in Action

Bob Danzig, who would one day head the Hearst Newspaper Group, learned a humbling lesson about leadership early in his career.

Danzig was just starting as an advertising director for a large food store chain. While he may have been eager to begin working on large-scale sales campaigns, his boss had other plans for Danzig's first day—Danzig spent the day inventorying jars of baby food with the head of the company.

"I do that job," his boss told him, "and everyone notices."

The best leaders lead by example. Let those around you see the care and integrity with which you treat even the smallest or most tedious jobs, and they'll follow your example.

Let us set an example for our kindred.
(Judith 8:24)

Almighty and Eternal Lord, help me to be a leader in both word and deed.

Racing to Victory Junction

On May 12, 2000, 19-year-old NASCAR driver Adam Petty died when his car slammed into a wall. And, while his father, racing champion Kyle Petty, finished the season in his son's car, grief made him essentially put his life on hold.

By the following year, though, Kyle Petty decided to proceed with a free camp for seriously ill children that he and his son had talked about starting. With the encouragement and financial support of many members of the NASCAR community, the Victory Junction Gang Camp in North Carolina opened its doors to hundreds of children in 2004.

Fellow driver Tony Stewart said, "When you look at the camp, you can see this is all about Kyle and his wife Pattie. They lost their son, and now they're doing something positive in his memory."

Grief is a terrible burden. Yet doing good for others may make the pain and loss more bearable.

Jesus began to weep. ...Then Jesus, again greatly disturbed, came to the tomb. Jesus said, "Take away the stone." (John 11:35,38,39)

Show me how to ease the anguish of the bereaved, Spirit of Peace.

Moms and Inmates

Operation: MOM is underway!

Volunteer mothers from the San Francisco Bay area work side by side with about 50 inmates from San Quentin State Prison—all military veterans—to wrap care packages filled with snacks, toiletries, disposable cameras and more for U.S. troops around the world.

Dotty Selmeczki founded Operation: MOM with Gloria Godchaux when, after September 11, 2001, Godchaux's son left for active duty with the U.S. Marine Corps. These mothers also meet monthly to share feelings about loved ones and to encourage each other to be strong.

With more than 15,000 care packages sent to date, Selmeczki couldn't be more proud. "This is something that comes from the heart," she said.

The gifts we give, no matter the size, are best when offered with love.

God loves a cheerful giver. (2 Corinthians 9:7)

May Your love make me strong and ease my fears, Master.

Brighten Someone's Day

"I love to feel the sunshine on my face. ...I love to sit outside and watch people walk by; I love to be hugged by someone." Because Lydia Burdick couldn't find an adult book to share with her mother who had Alzheimer's Disease, she wrote one with simple upbeat sentiments and pleasing pictures.

Looking at the book, *The Sunshine on My Face*, triggered memories and conversation. Burdick was able to share enjoyable moments reading with her mother before she died.

"I said, 'Do you like to feel the sunshine on your face?' And she looked at me and she lit up. Her smile was bigger than I had seen in years. She said, 'I do! I do!'

"I had my mom back in a way that I hadn't for a long time."

Communicate with those you love—with words, a touch, but always from the heart.

Those who respect their mother are like those who lay up treasure. (Sirach 3:4)

Inspire those who work with the elderly, Ancient of Days.

From Pain to Promise

Sometimes, the suffering people endure can inspire them to reach out to others.

Jeannie Hanneman was a little girl when her mother endured a difficult pregnancy, only to give birth to a son who died within days. Later, Hanneman and her husband went through years of infertility before their daughters were born, one with serious birth defects. As a parish director of family ministry, she saw the pain many people experienced from a variety of childbearing related issues.

That's when Hanneman started Elizabeth Ministries. Volunteers in hundreds of church-related groups offer comfort, advice and practical support for those having difficulties related to pregnancy, infertility, adoption, special needs, miscarriage or a child's death.

Perhaps the difficulties in your life have equipped you to assist others. Do all you can. It could mean all the difference in the world to someone.

The gifts He gave were...to equip the saints for the work of ministry, for building up the body of Christ. (Ephesians 4:11,12)

Child of Nazareth, guide us in serving others with all the wisdom that You have given us.

India's Child Genius

Shubham Prakhar grew up in the poorest and most dangerous region in India. There's a murder approximately every four hours in his home state of Bihar, and nearly daily kidnappings for ransom. Both of Shubham's parents were unemployed. Things could hardly be more hopeless for the young boy.

Yet when he was twelve, Shubham participated in a TV quiz competition and was dubbed "India's Child Genius." He beat out the other 16,000 entrants by studying for hours a day in the months leading up to the competition.

"I read 70 books, including classics, between April and August," he explained.

Shubham's prizes included a CD-ROM of the complete *Encyclopedia Britannica,* a glass trophy, a set of pens—and a cash prize of 1 million rupees. He now hopes to study and become a scientist or an engineer.

Even in the direst of circumstances, hope and hard work can turn things around.

**All things work together for good.
(Romans 8:28)**

Lord, let me see how I can be more positive in my life.

Shhh...

For many of us, it is difficult to "bite our tongues"–to keep silent for even a few moments. This is especially true if we believe we have something urgent to say.

Consider then activist John Francis' decision to remain silent for 17 years. Francis had a big message to convey–the importance of working for world peace–but as a protest against violence, he refrained from speaking for nearly two decades. He broke his silence only to embark on a more aggressive effort to encourage others to work for peace.

By adhering to an unusual, challenging and courageous path, Francis inspired thousands of people to slow down, listen and think about the choices they make in their own lives.

In silence, one can find volumes of wisdom. Take time to enjoy solitude and quiet whenever possible. It might allow you the room and opportunity to hear the true voice of your own spirit.

In quietness and in trust shall be your strength. (Isaiah 31:15)

Holy Spirit, bathe me in the peace and calm of Your presence.

The Thrill of the Hunt

As a child, Jeremy Irish loved to read stories about quests for hidden treasures.

As an adult, he founded Groundspeak, to provide an opportunity to participate in modern-day treasure hunts. Using both 21st century gadgetry and the age-old desire to explore new worlds, Groundspeak organizes treasure hunts, called "geocaches." An estimated 750,000 people currently participate, relying on global positioning system coordinates (GPS) and traversing nature trails and city streets. Their goal is to find "caches" —more than 100,000 active caches hidden in over 200 countries—that have been planted by fellow enthusiasts.

Although the prizes are often a child's toy or a good luck charm, participants say it's the thrill of the hunt that keeps them coming back for more.

How can you nurture your soul to keep the joy and wonder of a childlike nature?

Unless you change and become like children, you will never enter the Kingdom of heaven. (Matthew 18:3)

Help me remain young at heart, Child of Nazareth.

A Tapestry of Patience, Quality and Beauty

Every day Iranian carpet maker Kazem Karimi's meticulously weaves fine silk threads into carpets in his home. While at the half-way point of his labor on one rug, nine months, Karimi says "God is with the patient." Meanwhile a carpet factory churns out 3 million square meters (32 million square feet) of patterned industrial rugs every year.

Karimi's own family cannot enjoy these beautiful handmade carpets, since "they all go for export." Because of competition from rug factories and the time needed to hand-weave on single rug looms, small workshops have become hard to maintain. They can only supplement income.

Still, nothing can match the beauty of a person's individual, hand-crafted work. Even the imperfections of a hand-crafted item add to its beauty through uniqueness.

Support the individually-owned businesses in your community. They help keep a human touch in daily life.

I will give you my support. (2 Samuel 3:12)

Creator, inspire those who labor at lathe and loom to create reflections of Your loveliness.

Ways to Reduce Stress

Stress is an inevitable part of life, but too much causes multiple health and psychological problems. Throughout history, religious and health practitioners have suggested ways to achieve peace and serenity.

At the Om Spa in Chicago for example Christina Burns, a meditation instructor, suggests sitting straight backed in a chair or cross-legged on the floor. Next, relax your facial muscles. Then choose a short phrase to repeat aloud in a soft voice. Here are some examples: "I am happy to have a healthy body," "I possess great potential," or "May I grow in universal kindness and compassion."

Finally, inhale and exhale deeply, slowly, consciously over and over for as few as five minutes or as many as 15. Repeat your chosen prayer or phrase whenever you become distracted.

Take a few minutes today. Choose to relax!

He said to them, "Come away to a deserted place all by yourselves and rest a while." (Mark 6:31)

Inspire and guide our times of relaxation and reflection, Holy Spirit.

All People and Breeds Welcome

It seems a small church in Vermont takes the principle "all are welcome" to a new level regarding its congregation.

Dog Chapel, a church that sits atop a lovely hill in northeast Vermont (aptly named "Dog Mountain"), welcomes all humans and their dogs who seek fellowship with others and with God.

The little white building and stately steeple could be mistaken for a 19th century New England church, but on closer inspection, the church is anything but traditional. Inside, black labs and golden retrievers wander around or sit quietly, next to their owners, during a service. Even the interior structure reflects the congregation's philosophy: the chapel's pews feature carvings of dogs created by the chapel's founder Stephen Huneck.

Whatever you think about a chapel that welcomes dogs, there's no doubt that God loves all His creatures and expects us to care for them. After all, we are not only God's stewards, we are His children.

Brothers and sisters...agree with one another, live in peace; and the God of love and peace will be with you. (2 Corinthians 13:11)

God, help me find peace and unity with others. We were not meant to be alone.

Something's Gained and Something's Lost

Call it charming and quaint or old fashioned and antiquated.

For a long time, the clocks in New York's Grand Central Station were out of sync. A rider would see different times displayed by the clock on a train platform and above the main information booth.

This haphazard situation was maddening to commuters who needed to catch trains. It also annoyed those who were aware of the historical role railroads played in the establishment of standard times zones across the country.

But now satellite-based technology allows transportation centers, TV and radio stations, utilities, and the like, to synchronize to an official atomic clock, down to the nanosecond.

No question, technology improves many things. Still, there's something to be said for charming imperfection.

There is no one on earth so righteous as to do good without ever sinning. (Ecclesiastes 7:20)

Liberate us, Jesus, from inhuman perfectionism.

Anton's Gift

When Autumn Alexander-Skeen took her then four-year old son, Anton, for a car ride one sunny day in Seattle, she made sure to secure his seatbelt. State law at that time allowed a child of Anton's size to use an adult seat belt.

But when her SUV skidded off the road and rolled over, the adult seatbelt did not adequately secure little Anton. He died. Had he been secured in a child booster seat, he might have survived.

Alexander-Skeen overcame her shattering grief by working to save other children's lives. She wrote letters to her state legislators, and informed other parents of the perils of relying on adult seatbelts to protect small children. Resulting state and federal regulations have improved children's safety in cars.

Autumn Alexander-Skeen took a personal tragedy and made something positive out of it—for others.

However difficult your own circumstances may be, you can find a way to do good.

Help the weak. (1 Thessalonians 5:14)

God, bless those who have the compassion, strength and faith to dedicate their lives to helping others.

The Happiness Factor

The citizens of Bhutan, a small country nestled high in the Himalaya Mountains, consider themselves some of the happiest people on earth.

No wonder. Theirs is the only country in the world to make happiness a national goal. In fact, when measuring national development they've set aside the usual economic factors to focus on "gross national happiness." This unique approach measures satisfaction with things like the environment, national culture and democratic governance.

Realizing that material wealth doesn't necessarily bring contentment or fulfillment, researchers and think tanks around the world have started their own happiness studies. The quality of social relationships, job stability, democratic institutions and solid human rights directly affect citizens' happiness.

Looking for happiness? Improve your relationships with family, friends and neighbors. And, above all, don't forget God.

Solitary individuals...(ask) "For whom am I toiling...and depriving myself of pleasure?" This also is vanity and an unhappy business. Two are better than one. (Ecclesiastes 4:8-9)

May I find happiness in friendship with You, Beloved Lord, and with other people.

Faith, Courage and Shelter

"We barely had food," said Angela Lariviere, whose family moved 39 times in her first 10 years, "but we always had that basis of faith that carried us."

Although her mother had physical and mental illnesses that caused the family's instability, Lariviere says, "we were always taught to share what we had."

Her family also prayed a particular scripture verse daily: "God did not give us a spirit of cowardice, but rather a spirit of power and love and of self-discipline." (2 Timothy 1:7)

Lariviere took these lessons into adulthood, earning her college degree while caring for her mother and siblings. Now married with two children, she is coordinator of the Youth Empowerment Project of the Ohio Coalition on Homelessness and Housing. She says, "As long as you keep your eye on God's purpose, you'll always find the right path."

Do we keep our eyes on God and God's plans for us?

I know the plans I have for you, says the Lord, plans for your welfare and not for harm, to give you a future with hope. (Jeremiah 29:11)

Reassure me, Lord, that at each moment I am where You want me to be.

Civility in the Office

According to three studies conducted over eight years by the University of South California's Marshall School of Business, you may be among the 80 percent of employees who "believe they get no respect at work" or the 20 percent who experience "incivility on a weekly basis."

Workplace incivility has its consequences: decreased performance, inability to concentrate, decreased creativity, decreased company loyalty, increased turnover. 1 in 8 employees cite on-going rudeness as the reason for resigning.

Managers are affected as well. It costs the average Fortune 1000 executive seven work weeks each year "mediating worker disputes."

A song played on "easy listening" radio stations includes the spelled-out word R E S P E C T. Make that your mantra when dealing with your fellow employees, with your subordinates, and with your supervisors. You deserve respect—and so do all those around you.

Love does no wrong to a neighbor; therefore, love is the fulfilling of the law. (Romans 13:10)

How can we foster mutual respect in the workplace, on the job, everywhere, Jesus?

A Friend in Need

Jody Winter longed for the days when she had been able to live a full life. At age 30, she suddenly developed epilepsy, a disease whose seizures can happen anywhere, anytime.

Pretty soon, Winter's *fear* of having a seizure in public actually overshadowed the impact of the disease itself. As a result, her life became more narrow, her world more restricted.

It took the encouragement and persistence of a special friend to help Jody Winter get back to the business of living. Whenever she seemed to be giving up, her friend Betty would encourage her to see the reasons why she *could* accomplish something, rather than why she couldn't.

Today, Jody Winter's seizures are better controlled through medication, and she has regained much of her former independence.

Friends celebrate each other's wins, and grieve each other's losses. A true friend never gives up, even when the going gets rough.

A true friend sticks closer than one's nearest kin. (Proverbs 18:24)

Dear God, may I remember that friendship is a blessing we should never take for granted. Please bless my friends.

Reviving the Past Through Music

Rodney Regier has nothing against modern-day pianos. It's just that compared to a 19th century Viennese fortepiano, the modern descendant of this instrument and its cousin, the harpsichord, simply isn't, as he says, "musically superb."

Regier is one of only a handful of people in the world today who actually build early keyboard instruments. Using mahogany, spruce, ash and pear wood, he models his fortepianos after the early 1800 originals, which had been built for Beethoven, Chopin, Schubert and Brahms.

While Regier has built harpsichords, which he also plays, the fortepiano is truly his favorite. The sound is "rhapsodic" to his ears, as is the process of creating these, now nearly forgotten, musical instruments. "It's something I eat and breathe," he says of his work.

What greater blessing than to be so enraptured with one's daily toil!

It is God's gift that all should...take pleasure in all their toil. (Ecclesiastes 3:13)

Carpenter of Nazareth, Jesus, redirect my sights to what truly inspires my soul.

Beneath the Granite and Water

In May 2004, a memorial to honor the 16 million men and women who served in the United States armed forces in World War II was unveiled on Washington DC's National Mall.

The memorial, with granite walls, waterfalls and fountains, is majestic in scope and splendid in design. Beyond the surface of the bronze panels, stone inscriptions and custom-made flagpoles marked with emblems of each division of the armed forces, lies the meaning of the memorial· unprecedented sacrifice.

One viewer regarded the memorial as a "giant thank-you note" to the soldiers, sailors and marines who died in World War II.

Help preserve the memory of all those who paid "the last full measure of devotion"–their lives–in the name of freedom.

In days to come...they shall beat their swords into plowshares, and their spears into pruning hooks; nation shall not lift up sword against nation, neither shall they learn war any more. (Isaiah 2:2,4)

Prince of Peace, console the families of deceased service men and women.

Some Instructions for Life

These suggestions were offered by the Dalai Lama at the start of this millennium. They are worth considering.

- Great love and great achievements involve great risk.
- When you lose, don't lose the lesson.
- Follow the three R's: respect for self, respect for others and responsibility for all your actions.
- Don't let a little dispute injure a great friendship.
- When you realize you've made a mistake... correct it.
- Open your arms to change, but don't let go of your values.
- Live a good, honorable life.
- Share your knowledge.
- Be gentle with the earth.
- Once a year, go some place you've never been before.

Whatever you do, be sure to light candles of faith, hope and love with your life. And don't forget to light candles of peace, as well.

Blessed are those who hunger and thirst for righteousness...Blessed are the peacemakers. (Matthew 5:6,9)

Abide with me in dark and difficult times, Good Shepherd.

A Man of Courage and Caring

When Douglas Bader died in 1982, his obituary in the London Times called him "the personification of RAF heroism during the Second World War."

His life was unusual. In 1931, the 21-year-old Royal Air Force officer cracked up his plane while demonstrating flying acrobatics. Both legs had to be amputated.

Reinstated in the RAF in 1939, Bader, wearing artificial legs, earned a reputation for courage and leadership which earned him several decorations. He was shot down over France, but made numerous escape attempts.

After the war, he helped disabled veterans, especially amputees. He was knighted for these services in 1976. Shortly before Douglas Bader died he talked about his legacy.

He said, "I want to be remembered so that other people, when they talk about me, smile. That's how I want to be remembered. The thing is this: I want to leave warmth behind."

Let's all leave warmth behind.

Has the Lord as great delight in burnt offerings and sacrifices, as in obeying the voice of the Lord? Surely, to obey is better than sacrifice, and to heed than the fat of rams. (1 Samuel 15:22)

Almighty God, grant me the will to serve You with my whole life, my whole being.

Artists of Life

Are some people naturally kinder and more loving than others? Probably. But that does not mean that we can't nurture our own efforts to be gracious and compassionate.

Author and screenwriter Myles Connelly wrote that "Everybody at one time or another has known people, strangers, relatives or friends who have changed the quality of the day for others. ...The shining quality of goodness radiates from them, from their mere presence. All these, humble and unaware, carry with them the kindness and generosity of their lives. These are the greatest artists. They practice the highest of arts—the art of living, the art of life itself."

That's not a bad goal for all of us—to strive to excel in the art of living—not just for our own sake, but for a world full of people who need all the good we have to give.

Give alms. Make purses for yourselves that do not wear out, an unfailing treasure in heaven. (Luke 12:33)

O Generous God, Your bounty and compassion are greater than we will ever comprehend. Show me how to reveal Your blessings to others as well as myself.

James Forman: Activist, Pioneer, Hero

James Forman, one of the most influential figures of the civil rights movement of the 1960s died in 2005, at age 76.

As a black man growing up in segregated Mississippi, Forman knew that something had to be done to ensure equal rights for all. In a 1996 interview, Forman recalled nearly being lynched when he was 8 years old for not saying "Yes Ma'am" to a white clerk.

In 1961, Forman became an executive secretary of the Student Nonviolent Coordinating Committee (SNCC) wherein he planned and played a part in several major civil rights demonstrations.

Forman often referred to the battle for civil liberties as a people's movement. SNCC brought the fight to where it was needed most, becoming the first group of professional civil rights workers most small Southern towns had ever met.

Much can be learned from James Forman's lifelong struggle to spread God's message of peace.

In passing judgment on another you condemn yourself. (Romans 2:1)

Remind us, Abba, that we should love each other as You love all of Your children, equally.

The Point of Pain

When you suffer or care for a loved one in agony, it's natural to want the pain to stop.

But those with a rare disorder known as CIPA, or congenital insensitivity to pain with anhidrosis, know the problems that can result. The condition interferes with the development of nerve fibers that carry sensations of pain, heat or cold to the brain. Those with the disorder cannot feel normal aches and pains; nor do they perspire.

The parents of one little girl with CIPA must check her food to make sure she won't burn her mouth. They must be vigilant about infections and illness. The school nurse examines her for injuries after every recess.

"Pain's there for a reason," says the child's mother. "It lets your body know something's wrong and it needs to be fixed. I'd give anything for her to feel pain."

The human body is an amazing gift from God. Use yours well.

The Lord God formed man from the dust of the ground, and breathed into his nostrils the breath of life. (Genesis 2:7)

Bless my body, mind and soul, O Father. May I praise and serve You with my whole being.

Listening for and Responding to God's Call

Jean Vanier's goal was to live a life of poverty.

Raised in Switzerland by parents who were considered for sainthood because of their devotion to God, Jean absorbed his parents' fervor for the work of Jesus.

After a stint in the navy, Jean joined a small lay community in a poor area of Paris. It proved to be another step in his lifelong quest to "follow Jesus, and live the way of the gospel."

Taking his pursuit even further, he left a promising academic career and a comfortable life to serve people with disabilities. Today, the organization he founded, L'Arche, is an international association of 130 communities in 30 countries that serve those with developmental disabilities.

How do you define serving God? Helping others? Donating to charities? Extraordinary sacrifice? Simple acts of love at home, at work, in your neighborhood?

Jesus...saw a man called Matthew sitting at the tax booth; and He said to him, "Follow Me." And he got up and followed Him. (Matthew 9:9)

Jesus, You gave Your life so that I may live. How thankful I am for Your indescribable love!

Graze Your Way to a Beautiful Lawn

Contrary to popular myth, the image of a tin-can eating goat couldn't be further from the truth. Goats instead prefer to graze on weeds, and sociologist Jim Guggenhime has the successful business venture to prove it.

Thanks to an innovative nature and a keen eye for opportunity, Guggenhime sensed a growing demand for safe, natural weed control from a largely untapped and diverse market of potential clients, ranging from country clubs to private homes.

With a herd of just over 200 goats, Jim launched Nip It in the Bud, a business that supplies and oversees browsing goats which are employed as bio-control agents. They graze away to rid lawns of tough weeds, shrubs, leaves and twigs.

Opportunity may not always knock loudly, but with a bit of creativity and your own unique perspective, you may be able to hear it tap gently at your door.

Whenever we have an opportunity, let us work for the good of all. (Galatians 6:10)

Lord God, thank You for the countless opportunities that cross my path each and every day. Help me to make the most of them!

That Japanese Beat

When you think salsa dancing, do you usually think…Japan?

The provocative dancing style is often associated with images of passionate Latinos and Latinas, as opposed to the more normally reserved Japanese. Yet salsa had been causing quite a stir in Japan, becoming the hobby of choice for many people in their 20s and 30s.

"Japanese are shy, and they tend to keep things pent up inside," says Mayumi Iida, an office worker in her late 20s who's become a salsa aficionado. "Listening to the music and moving the body is really liberating."

You never know when something from a culture not your own might attract your interest. The world is full of wonders–why not investigate some of them?

The prophet Miriam, Aaron's sister, took a tambourine in her hand; and all the women went out after her with tambourines and with dancing. And Miriam sang…to the Lord. (Exodus 15:20-21)

Lord, help me to experience the world with an open mind.

Making a Big Difference in Little Ways

When London doctor John Hughes-Games died from leukemia at the age of 77, one of his final requests was quite unusual.

"I would really like to leave some money to have these windows cleaned," he told his wife, Susan, referring to the grimy windows in the Bristol hospital where he was treated before his death.

Hughes enjoyed seeing the sky and watching the birds fly by during his illness, but the dirty windows often denied him even that simple pleasure. He didn't want future patients to have the same experience. In his death notice, his family asked that any donations be sent to a window-cleaning fund for the center.

Making a difference in the life of others sometimes can be as simple as...well, washing a window! Find little ways to improve the lives of those around you.

The good person out of the good treasure of the heart produces good. (Luke 6:45)

Spirit of Hope, give me the grace to anticipate the needs of others, no matter how small.

Oops! Can I Take That Back?

Have you ever wished you could retrieve that e-mail you wrote in haste or in anger to a friend or co-worker?

Since the advent of e-mail, most of us have experienced "e-mail regret." Kieran Vogel sent one too many regretful e-mail, and decided to design a software program to address the problem.

Vogel describes Bigstring.com as "the world's first fully-recallable, erasable e-mail" program. It works by establishing a link to all e-mails from a particular sender. Later the sender can "call back" or even destroy an e-mail message, even if it's been opened or forwarded by the recipient.

While such an invention seems handy, we can't apply it to the words we speak. Once spoken, our words can not be taken back. Take care choosing your words. Words can hurt if not chosen carefully.

A word fitly spoken is like apples of gold in a setting of silver. (Proverbs 25:11)

May I practice discretion and prudence when speaking with others, Eternal Trinity.

Art the Herald Angels Sing

While attending graduate school at the University of Illinois at Chicago, Lucinda Naylor created a series of paintings in which hands hold chalice-like coffee cups.

Naylor, now the artist-in-residence for the Basilica of St. Mary in Minneapolis, is extremely talented at finding the sacred in everyday situations.

"It makes us appreciative of the beauty in the world. Art and Catholicism go hand in hand," said Naylor.

At the Basilica, the artist creates large, vibrant pieces that hang from the heights of the church. Many parishioners find her work breathtaking. However, Naylor insists that the message of her art must not be overlooked.

"It's not just there to look pretty; it's there to add meaning to your worship experience."

If we open our eyes and our minds, we all can find the spiritual in even the most ordinary things.

When I look at your heavens...the moon and the stars that you have established; what are human beings...Yet You have made them a little lower than God. (Psalm 8:3-4,5)

May I know Your beauty, Holy God, through the enjoyment of nature, music and art.

Come, Sail Away

Jim Gladson knows that a successful person is not always the one who goes to a good college and makes a lot of money.

That's why he started taking troubled pre-teens aboard his schooner, the Irving Johnson—to teach them what they don't learn in school.

"What do you do with dysfunctional kids and how do you stop building them?" Gladson asks rhetorically.

In 1973 Gladson answered his question by turning his large sailing vessels into floating classrooms for poor children from high-crime neighborhoods. He hoped that all the hard work that goes into maintaining a ship would teach the children valuable lessons in team-work and self-worth.

By 1998, 26 middle schools, funded by the Port of Los Angeles, had committed to 260 sailing days a year. And since his program began, Gladson has had more that 10,000 kids crew his ships.

Hard work and creativity solve most problems.

Take care that you do not despise one of these little ones; for...in heaven their angels continually see the face of My Father in heaven. (Matthew 18:10)

Thank You, Holy Spirit, for inspiring those who care for troubled youths.

Love's Great Power

If you think love is simply an emotion, think again. It can be a force of heaven. Whatever love we have for ourselves, for others and for God, we love because God first loved us.

Here are some thoughts about love:

- Love is pleasant when it would be easy to be irritable;
- Love listens even when it's not convenient;
- Love speaks kindly of those whom others belittle;
- Love draws out the best from those who often fail;
- Love delights in giving attention rather than in attracting it;
- Love respects the other's point of view without necessarily accepting it;
- Love knows how to disagree without becoming disagreeable;
- Love rejoices at the success of others instead of being envious;
- Love avoids causing unnecessary pain even when its difficult.

How simple love is – until we try to live love.

Let love be genuine...love one another with mutual affection. (Romans 12:9,10)

Help me ponder how Your Heart was broken for love of me, Compassionate Savior.

Lord Only Knows

"When I can't solve a problem and need help, I turn to God," says scientist Tom Ippoliti.

At the University of St. Thomas in St. Paul, Minnesota, Ippoliti teaches his students to work as diligently on their molecular experiments as he does. "If I could detect cancer with a molecule that gave off light that would be my goal. I would enjoy that," said Ippoliti.

Research by Ippoliti and his students have helped in the development of color-changing sunglass lenses and balloon catheters used in arteries. And they did it by ignoring the supposed age-old battle between religion and science. "I have an unusual sense of creativity and I attribute that to God," said Ippoliti.

Reason and intelligence are not the opposite of faith but faith's support. In fact, reason and intelligence have been given to us by God. It is up to us to use them for God's glory and human benefit.

**Every good tree bears good fruit.
(Matthew 7:17)**

Thank You, Holy Wisdom, for my intelligence and intellectual curiosity.

Love Speaks Volumes

Writing about her infant daughter and octogenarian father, in *Family Circle* magazine Elizabeth Cohen poignantly illustrates the power of love.

Her father, diagnosed with Alzheimer's Disease, is slowly loosing his grip on language while her young daughter Ava is slowly strengthening her grasp on it.

"The part of him that can do things expands in her presence. Around her he is a person who knows things...and he knows he can teach her," Cohen writes.

"'Do it like this,' he says. He wets their hands and they wash together, scrubbing up to their elbows in bubbles. 'This is how to wash.' She giggles. She loves bubbles. She is beginning to love him."

Cohen says she likes to think "that instead of him losing the abilities to speak, to walk and to negotiate the world, he is giving them to (Ava)." What a wonderful gift!

Help your father in his old age, and...even if his mind fails, be patient with him; because you have all your faculties do not despise him. (Sirach 3:12,13)

Author of Life, inspire doctors and scientists investigating the causes, preventions and cures for disease.

Underground Road to Freedom

Most of us have heard about the Underground Railroad of the 1800s. Yet, do you know how much the railroad accomplished?

The Underground Railroad was not a physical railroad, but a loose network of people and places that helped African-American slaves escape to freedom. Out of the millions of African-Americans enslaved between 1640 and 1865, the Railroad rescued an estimated 100,000 men, women and children from slavery.

Says one historian, "The Underground Railroad is actually a metaphor for the ongoing struggle for freedom."

Slavery still exists in many parts of the world today. Seek ways to help those who are denied their freedom.

You shall not deprive a resident alien or an orphan of justice; you shall not take a widow's garment in pledge. Remember that you were a slave in Egypt and the Lord your God redeemed you. (Deuteronomy 24:17-18)

Father, remember those men, women and children who live in bondage; bring them liberty.

From Service to Scholarship

"It used to be that when you sent in your scholarship application, you listed that you were ...the head of the clean-up drive and a volunteer fireman," said 73-year-old-Alabama heiress Mignon C. Smith. "But if you look today, many scholarships are wholly based on grade points and test scores."

That is a practice that Smith is trying to correct. She has begun a $10 million scholarship program that provides full tuition, room, board and books for 10 Alabama students who attend any of the state's four-year colleges. Unlike most scholarship programs, however, this one rewards students who have devoted themselves to community and family service, despite low grades.

"It's for the child raised by a single mom who's been helping with siblings and doing volunteer work in a nursing home," said Ahrian Davis Tyler, a lawyer who helped Smith establish the foundation.

Remember that sometimes even the most unlikely candidate deserves a chance.

Do not judge and you will not be judged. (Luke 6:37)

Remind me, Holy Spirit, to advance the well-being of those in need.

Hey, Why Didn't I Think of That?

Did you know that the world's largest private bank, the Bank of America, began as the Bank of Italy? It was founded by Amadeo Giannini at the turn of the 20th Century to help poor immigrants in San Francisco who were refused loans by major banks.

And the first form of the bra in America was created by Russian immigrant Ida Rosenthal because the steel used to rib corsets was needed elsewhere during World War I and the flapper look which followed didn't suit all women.

And while Jean Nidetch did not create the diet that helped her and her friends lose pounds in the early 1960's, her method of meeting and discussing progress and problems with other dieters began the now multi-billion-dollar Weight Watchers program.

One simple innovation can re-shape the way future generations think about the world. Look back at the changes made in the past to truly appreciate your present.

Hezekiah fortified his city, and brought water into its midst; he tunneled the rock with iron tools, and built cisterns for the water.
(Sirach 48:17)

Lord, fill me with Your wisdom so I can do something which will be cherished by future generations.

Rice of Life

To some, Kapecs Vicente's rice fields might look like any other. To agriculturalists, however, they represent a breakthrough in farming.

Vicente used his love and knowledge of agriculture to help develop new techniques in organic rice cultivation. Growing in his fields near Manila, the Philippines, one can find more than 1,500 native varieties of rice, many of which are endangered.

Today, he has expanded his reach to share his talent and knowledge with the world community. He works with several global organizations to empower farmers in developing organic crops, as a way to save both the environment and native rice varieties.

How can you help save the environment as well as rare plants, birds and animals?

Consider the lilies, how they grow: they neither toil nor spin; yet I tell you, even Solomon in all his glory was not clothed like one of these. (Luke 12:27)

Help those who work to protect the earth's treasures, God.

Change is the Only Constant

Julie Slough loved to run with her dad Wesley, a serious runner who competed in marathons. Although sometimes it was hard to keep up with him, she relished her "alone time" with her beloved father.

When he ran his first race after open-heart surgery, Julie watched him carefully. "I want you to run ahead and make the best time you can," he told her. Julie assumed the worst.

However, there was no defeat in her father's voice, only acceptance. "Maybe I needed to accept that there comes a time for every child to step away from her parents and move on," she reasoned.

Julie ran her personal best that day, with her father finishing shortly after her. "We're still running together," she prayed. "Thank you Lord."

Circumstances and people change. Accepting that is perhaps the wisest and most loving thing we can do for others, and ourselves.

I the Lord do not change. (Malachi 3:6)

Holy Spirit, help me accept the changes of my life with grace and poise.

Right On the Money

Do you know where and how the money you put in your bank account is used?

Are you fully informed on how your investments are put to work in the marketplace?

Socially responsible investing is a term used to describe a greater awareness among consumers regarding how and where investment firms, banks and the like use the dollars they invest. For example, investors can now choose from a growing variety of "ethical investment funds," which reassure people that their money is not being invested in industries which they find harmful, like tobacco, alcohol or arms.

Every dollar counts—especially if you want to promote peace and justice in the world. Gain a greater awareness of where your money goes, so your money can work for the greater good.

A man...entrusted his property to (his slaves); to one he gave five talents, to another two, to another one, to each according to his ability. (Matthew 25:14-15)

I need to be more responsible regarding the causes my money supports. Guide my efforts, Lord of all.

Facing Life with a Song

Life had been looking good for Theresa Sareo until that moment in June 2002 when an impaired driver ran her down in New York City. She lost her whole right leg.

With two CDs to her credit, the singer had been enjoying name recognition that helped guarantee a good turnout at her performances in Manhattan clubs.

That "was an assault on my life," Sareo said. But it was one from which she fought her way back, first writing down her feelings as poetry. The poetry-turned-lyrics spoke directly to the pain and grief of loss. It helped Sareo respond to her loss with hope.

The singer has also held out that hope to others, speaking to and leading support groups for those who have lost limbs.

In all the twists-and-turns of life, it's best to face each day with a hope-filled heart.

Hope for good things. (Sirach 2:9)

O Comforter, abide with me, protect me and send me Your love, today, always.

Summertime: Is the Living Easy?

Summer is supposed to be a relaxing time.

We are supposed to go on vacation. We are supposed to head outdoors and do all those things we were unable to do while stuck inside with cabin fever all winter. Except, of course, we can't forget all those summer chores, like painting the guest room so that out-of-town relatives can come and stay.

And if we don't accomplish everything, we have wasted time and let the days fritter away. Frankly, we probably need to do a lot more frittering. The origin of the word "fritter" means to break into small pieces. Shouldn't at least part of summer be about breaking life into small pieces?

Shouldn't we be able to spend as much time lying on the grass as mowing it without our conscience nagging that we're wasting time?

Let's fulfill our obligations, of course. But let's remember that life should be more than a long "to do" list.

Let the final word be: "He is the all." Where can we find the strength to praise Him? For He is greater than all His works. Awesome is the Lord. (Sirach 43:27-29)

Show us how to enjoy the beauty and special pleasures of each season, Bountiful Father.

Wise about Wealth

Preparing for old age includes many things, one of the most crucial being financial planning.

According to financial advisor Suze Orman, there are a few key precepts to remember when planning for your financial future.

First, don't assume you'll be "taken care of." Instead, take an active part in planning for your financial health as you age.

Second, maximize your use of retirement accounts, workplace retirement savings plans and the like.

Third, secure your own home. If possible, pay off as much of your mortgage as you can, particularly as you near retirement.

Finally, be realistic. Engage the help of a professional or trusted advisor to gauge how much money you will *really* need once you stop working. It may be more or less than you assume.

Wise planning is part of life. Do your best today.

If you gathered nothing in your youth, how can you find anything in your old age? (Sirach 25:3)

Father God, instill in me the wisdom necessary to make prudent life decisions.

Better Living through Curiosity

What makes some women thrive well into their 90s while others die young or suffer from debilitating diseases?

Besides genetics, a study by author David Snowdon, PhD shows that those who age best share optimism, gratitude and engagement in a variety of intellectual challenges.

The study revealed that those women who strived to maintain a sharp mind, and who embarked on intellectual pursuits and who took on complex mental tasks, such as writing prose or studying difficult subjects, were more likely to remain mentally alert into their 80s and 90s.

According to the proverb, "curiosity killed the cat," but it's a positive factor in keeping humans alive longer and healthier.

Listen to Me (you)...who have been borne by Me from...the womb; even to your old age... even when you turn gray I will carry you. I have made, and I will bear...and will save. (Isaiah 46:3-4)

Help me take care of both my mind and my body, Creator who knit me in my mother's womb. Both are Your gifts which You have entrusted to my care.

Unexpected Turns

Would you expect to find a former centerfold making a difference among the poor in Haiti?

After posing nude in *Playboy* as Miss May, 1983, Susie Scott Krabacher turned her back on the centerfold lifestyle. She became a Christian, married, and began looking for something more fulfilling in life. She found that while visiting Haiti. After spending her first night there in a lean-to with a family of 17 people, she decided to devote herself to helping Haitian children.

It wasn't easy. At first, she wasn't taken seriously. Thugs threatened her at gunpoint. But Krabacher stuck it out, and, over the years, her nonprofit foundation has built six schools, three orphanages and a hospital and raised millions of dollars.

"I was born to do this work," Krabacher says, "I was not put here to be a *Playboy* centerfold."

No matter where your life takes you, it's never too late to find meaning. Have you been willing to look for it lately?

A woman who fears the Lord is to be praised. (Proverbs 31:30)

Beloved Christ, help me to look for meaning in my life.

That's Music to My Ears!

There's nothing quite like music to soothe, calm and invigorate the human spirit. Some researchers, however, are convinced that it can have an equally powerful effect on the human body.

At the Exempla Good Samaritan Medical Center, patients can choose from over 9,000 musical selections to help speed their recoveries from a variety of illnesses and injuries. It's part of the Center's efforts to create a new, holistic healing environment in which patients can benefit from the music's healing properties.

Music can enhance learning, creativity, and, perhaps, healing. Make it habit to enjoy your favorite tunes on a regular basis. It just might help improve your quality of life.

**Wine and music gladden the heart.
(Sirach 40:20)**

Gracious Lord, thank You for the beautiful music of life—not only the song of people, but of all nature.

Soldiers, their Pets and their Choices

Military reservists, when called to active duty, know that daily life will change for them and their family members. For some, family includes their cats, dogs, fish and other pets.

A soldier who has to leave on short notice, might not have time to make plans for a pet. This can lead to troubling choices including abandoning or euthanizing pets. That's where Operation Noble Foster (operationnoblefoster.org), Military Pets Foster Project (netpets.org) and other groups come in. They match soldiers with families willing to care for pets until their owners return.

"Having my pets in foster care and knowing that I am coming back to them is extremely calming," said Aeyne Anne Dizicksa, a reservist stationed in Germany.

According to an article in *Newsweek Magazine,* "soldiers are asked to pick up food and vet bills (though most foster families decline the food money).

What can you do today to help others make good choices?

Give graciously to all the living. (Sirach 7:33)

Guide our efforts to help others, Merciful Savior.

Silence is Golden–And Productive

Eighteen-year old Brett Banfe knew he had a problem listening to others. "I'm embarrassed to say that I almost didn't listen to people when they spoke…I would wait for them to stop talking so I could give my opinion," he admits.

As a remedy, Brett decided to stop speaking for a full year. While his decision made the local newspapers, his choice resulted in an immeasurably personal effect.

"Now I understand commitment," he says. "It doesn't matter what you want, it's what you're committed to."

Try simply listening carefully, even if for just a few hours. Focus on your surroundings. Most of all, aim to listen twice as much as you speak.

Stand on the mountain…for the Lord is about to pass by….there was a…sound of sheer silence. When Elijah heard it, he wrapped his face in his mantle. (1 Kings 19:11,12-13)

I pray to hear Your small, still voice within me that guides me, Eternal Lord.

Feeling Rejected

It is heartbreaking but inevitable that parents will see their children experience rejection.

"The reality is, rejection's a part of life. As much as we'd like to shield our child from rejection, we can't," writes Susan Alexander Yates. "Our job is to prepare our child for life, not protect her from the pain of it."

Nevertheless, Yates suggests strategies parents can use to help their youngsters cope with their pain, anger and disappointment:

Consider the reason for rejection. For example, if youngsters are disqualified from sports teams for failing to practice, they need to face the legitimate consequences.

Offer perspective. Your children may be devastated by the loss of their first true love. Give them hope that "pain doesn't last forever."

Remind your children that they're not alone. Jesus also knew rejection. Go to Him and seek comfort and understanding in prayer.

The Lord honors a father above his children, and He confirms a mother's right over her children. (Sirach 3:2)

Jesus Christ, inspire parents as they help their children learn to cope with life, with rejection.

A Lesson in Faith

It is often said that people can find religion in the most unexpected of places. Dale Ahlquist found it in the work of the early-20th-century English writer G.K. Chesterton.

Ahlquist said he was originally drawn to the author's diversity: "Chesterton was truly an interdisciplinary author. He talked about everything and every subject you can imagine."

But it was the author's views on Catholicism that ultimately hooked Ahlquist. Raised a devout Baptist, Ahlquist decided to convert to Catholicism. He now uses the American Chesterton Society to enlighten people about both the British author and the Roman Catholic Church.

You will never know where openness to new ideas may lead you unless you try it.

I am the gate for the sheep. ...Whoever enters by Me will be saved, and will come in and go out and find pasture. (John 10:7, 9)

Holy Spirit, give me the courage to follow the Good Shepherd wherever He leads me.

Being an MVP

In professional sports, when a most valuable player award is given, it's no surprise when it goes to an athlete who helped get the team a championship. But what about someone whose team was at the bottom of the standings?

In 1987, baseball's National League MVP was Andre Dawson, a tireless player and team leader. His team? The Chicago Cubs, who finished the season at the bottom of their division. Why was he so valuable? Here's an example:

In a game the Cubs were leading with a score of 11-1, Dawson kept diving for fly balls with his usual energy and speed. When he was asked why he bothered, he said, "Because the ball was in play."

Whether we think something is a sure thing or utterly hopeless, neither is a reason to stop trying. Our best should depend, not on circumstance, but on what we ask of ourselves.

Be persistent. (2 Timothy 4:2)

Spirit of Fortitude, when serious difficulties arise, it's so tempting to quit, to let somebody else deal with them. Encourage me to do the best I can, no matter what.

When a Quitter Is a Winner

From the time she was a very young girl growing up in Canada, Valérie Beauquier knew she wanted to be a performer.

Then one day she stopped trying–and she's never been happier. Quitting a dream can be one of the most difficult moves a person can make–but perhaps the bravest and smartest one.

At first glance, it seems unthinkable: Quitting is for losers, after all. But after some thought and lots of prayer, dropping the dream may be the best course of action.

For Beauquier, giving up on a stage career freed her to complete a radio and television course. Today she is a Radio Canada reporter and host.

It's not easy giving up on something you wanted. But with courage, honesty and patience, new dreams are always possible.

Are you clinging to something that's never going to happen? Go ahead, then, and dare to quit the dream.

When my soul was embittered...I was stupid and ignorant...Nevertheless I am continually with You; You hold my right hand. You guide me with Your counsel. (Psalm 73:21,22,23-24)

In times of disappointment, I look to You, Lord, to give me strength and hope.

Preserving Forests For The Future

When Clarence Petty speaks, people listen. And Petty has been speaking for nearly 100 years, on behalf of preserving his beloved Adirondack Mountains where he was born and still lives.

"I would be just as pleased if I could stand on the Capitol steps in Albany and look towards Montreal and not see a thing except wilderness," said Petty.

According to a local newspaper publisher, Petty is a maverick. "But he's not divisive because he's so respected." That's not to say there aren't people who disagree with his notion of environmental preservation and who are pushing for more development.

Petty says, "I would like to think that 300 years from now, people could come up here and find at least as much wild land as we've got now." That's six-million acres of mixed publicly and privately owned land.

What would you like to leave to future generations?

The good leave an inheritance to their children's children. (Proverbs 13:22)

Be the inspiration behind our conservation, Creator.

Kicking Cancer with the Karate Rabbi

When Rabbi Elimelech Goldberg was asked to serve as the director of a camp for children with cancer, he hesitated. Having lost his own daughter to the disease eight years earlier, he thought the experience would be too painful.

Fighting off his reservations, he took the post, using his own black belt in karate to help kids fight the disease. Goldberg discovered that the martial arts could inspire confidence in children who were physically and emotionally beaten by their illness. It even helped ease their physical pain. That led to his forming Kids Kicking Cancer, a charity that helps sick children cope via karate.

"We hear from doctors all the time that our kids need less morphine," says Goldberg. "We're even finding that children taking part are spending less time in the hospital."

In each of Goldberg's karate kids, we find a life lesson: no matter what we face, there's hope if we keep on kicking.

The Lord takes pleasure in those...who hope in His steadfast love. (Psalm 147:11)

Lord, give me strength and courage this day.

Patriotic Giving

Did you know that there are countless, sometimes surprising, ways to express your genuine patriotism through volunteer work?

If you're able, giving blood on a regular basis can help those in need in your community. Too, you may be helping injured veterans returning from the war in Iraq and elsewhere.

You can also call the Voluntary Service Office of your local VA center. Give your time to help those who have given their youth and health to protect your freedoms.

Or teach immigrants to speak and read English. That's an ideal way to build on the United States' diversity while helping newcomers get acclimated. It's also a good reminder that the United States is a nation of immigrants of every race and creed.

Thomas Jefferson said that "eternal vigilance is the price of liberty." Volunteer involvement with your community can be part of your payment.

Do good; seek justice, rescue the oppressed, defend the orphan, plead for the widow. (Isaiah 1:17)

Author of our liberties, remind us to uphold the dignity and rights of citizens, immigrants and visitors to the United States.

Links to the Past

Youngsters might appreciate history more if they got a feel–literally–for what archeologists do by sifting through dirt and searching for artifacts.

As part of a special project, ninth graders at Brooklyn's Science, Technology and Research High School (STAR), led by Dr. Arthur Bankoff, chairman of the Anthropology and Archeology Department at Brooklyn College, worked on an archeological dig on their own school grounds. Their high school had been built on the site of the 1787 Erasmus Hall Academy.

"The best way to experience (history) is to dig up things real people used. It gives them a measure of connection with the students that were here before."

Some kids were leery about getting dirty and working in the hot sun. That changed as they found an old watch, colorful pottery, shells, even a marble used during recess.

Those who do not know the past are bound to repeat it. Know the past. Embrace the present.

The advantage of knowledge is that wisdom gives life to the one who possesses it. (Ecclesiastes 7:12)

Prevent us, Holy Spirit, from repeating the mistakes of the past.

Being an Inspiration

Nelson Mandela will always be remembered for his heroic efforts against apartheid, along with his becoming South Africa's first black president. The octogenarian politician and activist is now taking on a new role–that of an amateur artist.

He has worked on a series of drawings that illustrate his memories of his 27-year imprisonment at Robben Island during the apartheid years. Mandela's pictures tell the tale of the horrific conditions he endured, but still manage to hint at his final triumph.

"He takes these desperate...scenes and yet every one is like a beacon of hope," says Roddy Sparks, who attended a charity exhibit where the works were unveiled. "He is such an inspiration...a symbol of reconciliation and hope."

God has given each and every one of us a special gift. Find your talent and use it to inspire others in every way possible.

So far as it depends on you, live peaceably with all. Beloved, never avenge yourselves, but leave room for the wrath of God. (Romans 12:18-19)

Lord, help me use my God-given talents for something that will glorify You and help others.

God's Time Out

Most people are good at doing things. From home to job to church to community activities, you probably do more than your share. But how are you at just being?

That's what rest, recreation and play are about: being rather than doing.

Think about the creation story from Genesis; that's the first place rest is mentioned. We read that God rested on the seventh day. But did God really need rest after making the universe? Perhaps, more than recuperating, God took time to revel and rejoice in His cherished creation.

Was God working or playing when He created His universe, His creatures, His people? For God, there probably is no difference, but we, His children, are still trying to figure it out for ourselves.

So, work at your work. Play at your play. Shed your tears. Enjoy your laughter. Now is the time of your life.

God blessed the seventh day and hallowed it, because on it God rested from all the work that He had done in creation. (Genesis 2:3)

Thank You, Beloved Creator, for granting us the ability to work and rest, to play and pray. Thank You, too, for time and eternity.

After Decades Apart, Friends for Life

In 1928, Herb Heilbrun and John Leahr—one white, one black—were part of the same third grade class in Cincinnati, Ohio. But they didn't play together.

Decades later, the two met at a reception honoring the Tuskegee Airmen, black pilots who fought in the U. S. Army Air Force during World War II.

"This lanky, white fellow comes up and puts his arms around me," Leahr recalls. The former classmates discovered that Leahr had flown cover for Heilbrun on two missions. These days, both men spend time together talking with schoolchildren about their wartime experiences and the importance of overcoming prejudice.

"Adlai Stevenson once praised Eleanor Roosevelt because she'd rather 'light a candle than curse the darkness,' and her glow has warmed the world,'" says Heilbrun. "Johnny and I aren't about to warm the world, but I think our story has certainly lit a few candles."

It's never too late to make a friend—or a difference.

Faithful friends are a sturdy shelter...a treasure ...beyond price...life-saving medicine. (Sirach 6:14,15,16)

Help me show Your love, Life-giving Spirit.

Try, Try Again...and Again...and Again...

There's an old saying about how when we fail at something, we should try, try again. But what about trying again 271 times?

That's how many times Seo Sang-moon took the academic part of his driver's license exam after failing it the first time.

Seo is an illiterate repairman in his 70s in a small, South Korean town. Unable to study the driver's manual so many people learn from, Seo took the exam, which is administered orally, as often as he could. With each failure, he learned a little more about the laws he needed to know to pass the test.

Failure affords us two opportunities: We can wallow in it, or we can learn from it. Keep trying—who knows what the rewards can be?

Those who look into the perfect law, the law of liberty, and persevere...being doers who act— they will be blessed in their doing.
(James 1:25)

Holy God, help me to have the dedication to persevere.

Maurice...Who?

Do you know Maurice Hilleman? You wouldn't be alone if you answered, "No."

But while Hilleman may not be as well known as, say, Louis Pasteur, his contributions to the world have been as important. Hilleman was a microbiologist who developed vaccines for chickenpox, mumps, measles, pneumonia and many other diseases. In fact, *The New York Times* once hailed him as having "probably saved more lives than any other scientist in the 20th century."

History is full of people whose names may not be well known, but who made valuable contributions to the world.

Choose a subject and investigate its history; or read about a person and see what you can learn.

A centurion (in Capernaum) had a slave whom he valued highly, and who was...close to death. ...Lord...I am not worthy to have you come under my roof. (Luke 7:2,6)

Blessed Trinity, help me to remember that we are all noteworthy in our own ways.

From Barrister to a Voice for the World

Peter Benenson was a barrister in London when he read a newspaper account of two young men who were arrested for toasting liberty in a café in a nation under the rule of a dictator. Benenson's first thought was to lodge a protest with that nation's embassy, but he was afraid that his one voice wouldn't be strong enough.

Instead, Benenson organized a one-year letter-writing campaign which he called, "An Appeal for Amnesty." The response was so overwhelming that, within a year, Benenson oversaw the formation on an organization that would later take the name Amnesty International.

Amnesty International is now the world's largest human rights group, with 1.8 million members and chapters in 64 countries. All this was born of one man's interest in a newspaper article, and his desire to make a difference in the world.

Each of us has power and potential. How we use them is up to us.

What good is it...if you say you have faith but do not have works? Can faith save you? So faith by itself, if it has no works, is dead. (James 2:14,17)

Lord, help me to recognize the powers and abilities I have, and how I can best use them to affect the world.

Gather Around the Table

When writer Brian Olszewski and his wife Ruth were young parents, they bought an Ethan Allen kitchen table to accommodate their family, including five children.

From the start "Ethan Allen," as the table became affectionately known, was treated with care because it was where they were a family together; where they ate, did homework, prayed, talked and played games together. "Ethan Allen" was there for the good times and the bad. And when the Olszewskis moved into a more spacious home, "Ethan Allen" went with them.

When the children grew up and left home, Brian and Ruth Olszewski bought a new table. But they set up "Ethan" in the basement, ready for family gatherings. They understood that this sturdy piece of wood represented the family's collective memory.

When we establish traditions in our family life, we plant the seeds of loving relationships and rich memories.

(Jesus) went down with them and came to Nazareth, and was obedient to them. ...And Jesus increased in wisdom and in years, and in divine and human favor. (Luke 2:51,52)

Son of Joseph and Mary, keep us focused on the things that matter.

"Cliché."

As managing editor of *Time* magazine, starting in the 1960's, Henry Grunwald would introduce bylines, create new sections and oversee a conversion to color photography.

When he started working at the magazine as a part-time copy boy, however, Grunwald was an Austrian refugee with an imperfect command of English. He threw himself into learning the language with enthusiasm, pestering reporters to watch them work.

That enthusiasm wasn't always welcome. One day, as Grunwald watched a reporter work on a story, the annoyed writer typed him a message: "Kid, if you don't cut this out, I'll break every bone in your body." Unimpressed, Grunwald responded: "Cliché." Grunwald continued to pester those around him, and to learn the skills he would need throughout his career.

Enthusiasm, perseverance and a healthy attitude are often the most important tools any of us can muster. What challenges are facing you in your life? How can you best meet them?

Happy are those who persevere. (Daniel 12:12)

Help me to meet all challenges that come to me, Lord.

Nature's Wide Selection

Scientists have often wondered why some animals are shy, when others of the same breed will greet anyone and anything that comes near them. Why doesn't nature select one personality type as a standard?

Ecologists in the Netherlands may have discovered the answer by studying the personalities and genetic makeup of birds. A variety of personalities, it seems, ensures that individuals of the species will survive, no matter how the conditions change. In times of plenty, more aggressive birds fight each other into smaller numbers, allowing shy birds to thrive. When times are lean, however, the aggressive birds are more successful in finding food.

In a way, the same sort of give-and-take may apply to humans. Each of us has traits and abilities that contrast and supplement those of others around us, enriching humanity as a whole. Appreciate those differences–they're part of the magic of life.

To each is given the manifestation of the Spirit for the common good. (1 Corinthians 12:7)

Father of all, help us to appreciate all those around us, and what they bring to our lives.

The Richest Material

Novelist Saul Bellow was walking down the street one day when he suddenly remembered a childhood friend. Chucky was "a wild talker," as Bellow recalled, "always announcing cheerfully that he had a super scheme." Bellow began to wonder what a novel told in Chucky's voice would sound like.

Bellow wrote that novel, and it became *The Adventures of Augie March,* a best-seller that established its author as a major American writer. Bellow was launched on an illustrious and critically-lauded career, which ended only with his death decades later. Throughout that span, Bellow often came back to the same source material for the wide range of characters he created–that of his own life and the people he met.

Life is full of the noteworthy people, moments and places that some think can be found only in fiction. Take a look at the world around you–who or what can you see in a new light?

How desirable are all His works and how sparkling they are to see! ...Who could ever tire of seeing His glory? (Sirach 42:22,25)

Show me how to appreciate the world, Eternal Creator, the work of Your hands.

Stressed? Try Prayer

Research from the University of Florida indicates that among older adults, prayer is more popular than exercise, vitamins and even humor for relaxation.

Perhaps that's because prayer puts us in touch with something greater than ourselves. Psychologist Dru Scott Decker notes, "Thinking you're at the center of the universe can be very stressful." So taking the focus off yourself shrinks your problems. Here are some thoughts on prayer:

Begin to pray slowly but consistently. Rev. James Keller, M.M., founder of The Christophers, wrote that with "three minutes a day you will find yourself talking to God with ease as you would a close friend."

Be still. Set your mind's clutter aside so you can pray and listen for the response.

Prayer is a process. Ask God to help you pray.

Prayer brings peace and, as Dr. Decker writes, "When you have more peace, you'll have less stress."

Lord, teach us to pray...He said to them, "When you pray, say: Father, hallowed be Your name. Your kingdom come. (Luke 11:1,2)

May I pray with a hopeful heart, Holy Spirit.

Saving the World with $10

While attending the 2002 World Summit on Sustainable Development in Africa, Adam Roberts was weighed down by data on the world's overwhelming poverty. Millions lack the basic components of healthy living–sufficient food, clean water, health care. Yet governments and institutions were slow to act or didn't at all. What could be done?

Roberts wrote to friends and family asking for just $10 a month which he'd use to directly eradicate some suffering in various parts of the world. With no overhead, no fees, and Roberts making sure every dime was spent on the project, what did they have to lose? That was the beginning of "The Ten Dollar Club."

The result: a well in Nicaragua; a electric generator and cribs for a Sierra Leone orphanage; medicines for Gambia's Bansang Hospital; mattresses and blankets for elderly Tibetans.

With the help of a few others, one person can make a world of difference.

Where your treasure is, there your heart will be also. (Luke 12:34)

How may I embrace the mission You have planned for me, Beloved God?

Living a Dream

George Lewis Scott was a young boy attending a school for the blind when, wanting more than a life of menial labor, he taught himself how to play the guitar.

In quick succession thereafter, he joined the glee club, spun off with two other members to form the Happy Land Jubilee Singers, and began touring the gospel music circuit in the American South. While on the road, the three young men signed on new members to become the Five Blind Boys of Alabama.

The group eventually shortened their name, and for six decades, the Blind Boys wowed audiences with, as one newspaper called them, "incendiary live shows." The group released 35 albums and won four Grammies.

George Scott could have easily taken the lot life handed him. Yet he had a dream and built a remarkable career on it.

What are your dreams, and how can you achieve them?

(Jacob) dreamed that there was a ladder set up on the earth, the top of it reaching to heaven... the Lord stood beside him. (Genesis 28:12,13)

I need to have the conviction to believe in my dreams. Guide me, Spirit of Faith.

Swollen Eye, Big Heart

Peter Scannell's battle to expose dubious trading techniques cost him his job, a brutal beating, and over $100,000 in lost wages. Still, Scannell refused to be silenced. He knew that telling the world the truth was the right thing to do, and he would not allow others to be stepped on.

Shortly after beginning his job at an investment firm, Scannell noticed a group of men making questionable trades with their stocks. Even after several attempts by these men to silence him, including an assault, Scannell still managed to go to the authorities, bringing the case to justice.

"I give all the credit in the world to Peter," said Massachusetts Director of Securities Matthew Nestor. "It's not easy to be the one person in the world who stands up and says, 'This is wrong.'"

Standing strong in the face of adversity is its own reward, especially when it helps others.

Keep up your courage. (Acts 27:25)

Help me stand fast when evil pushes me down, Lord God. For the sake of Your children, let my voice be Yours.

A True World Series

For years baseball has been called "The Great American Pastime," but is it really?

The belief that baseball's origin was in Cooperstown, NY, in 1839 was so undisputed that it was stated as fact in textbooks for years. The game's Hall of Fame is there. However, documents later placed the game's birthplace in Hoboken, NJ, in 1846, and then Pittsfield, MA, in 1791.

But Pittsfield might have to pass along its crown.

Drawings of men playing a baseball-type game in both 13th-century Spain and ancient Egypt exist, not to mention hundreds of references that place a similar game throughout various time periods on almost every continent.

Baseball, in its many incarnations, has certainly given pleasure throughout its long history.

Enjoy sports and exercise for yourself. They can be good for body and soul.

If you...know how to give good gifts...how much more will the heavenly Father give the Holy Spirit to those who ask Him! (Luke 11:13)

Take a moment to revel in all the glorious creations of the Lord and appreciate all of His gifts, even those we've yet to open.

The Ultimate Price

Angela Dawson made enemies–and received little help–as she struggled to rid her East Baltimore neighborhood of drug dealers.

Bricks were thrown through a kitchen window. She was assaulted. Fire bombs gutted her kitchen. Finally, early one morning the house was doused with gasoline and set on fire. The Dawsons and five of their six children were burned to death.

That pulled the community together. A neighborhood block watch was formed. Baltimore officials had vacant homes boarded up; alleys and vacant lots cleaned up. A recreation center was opened and summer and evening programs begun.

Her pastor, Rev. Iris Tucker, of Knox Presbyterian Church, said Dawson was "on a vigil."

Being "on a vigil" for any worthy cause is lonely and sometimes dangerous. Persevere. Change will come.

Let us run with perseverance the race that is set before us. (Hebrews 12:1)

May those who are troubled find needed help and not resort to drugs, Divine Physician.

Inventing a Genius

"Genius is one percent inspiration and ninety-nine percent perspiration."

Thomas Edison not only said those words but applied them to himself. The inventor who still holds the record for U.S. patents – 1093 – was nothing if not dogged in his perseverance.

Edison made Alexander Graham Bell's telephone practical and invented a phonograph and motion picture system. He not only made the first incandescent bulb in 1879, but also made it functional by figuring out how to build the dynamos, cable systems and connections. Within four years his first public generator was supplying 85 customers in New York. He was on the way to electrifying the world.

Perhaps his most intriguing invention was his method of inventing itself. His famous Menlo Park, New Jersey laboratory was the precursor of today's industrial research facility.

Remembering that determination counts even more than creativity might give us the confidence to keep going.

You need endurance. (Hebrews 10:36)

Guide me, Spirit of Wisdom, in doing my best, day by day by day.

Learning At Any Age

When the Kenyan government announced it would provide free primary schooling, enrollment grew from 5.9 million to 7.3 million practically overnight. Among the new students was Kimani Ngana Maruge, an 84-year-old widower and great-grandfather who had never had any kind of formal schooling.

Despite his age, Mr. Maruge convinced headmistress Jane Obinchu to allow him to enroll in the first grade at Kapkenduiywa Primary. Along with his classmates, many of who are more than 73 years his junior, he is learning to read and to do basic math.

"Let them who want to make fun of me do it," Mr. Maruge says. "I will continue to learn."

It's never too late to gain knowledge. True wisdom comes from realizing that no matter your age, you can always learn.

O the depth of the riches and wisdom and knowledge of God! How unsearchable are His judgments and how inscrutable His ways! (Romans 11:33)

Give me grace to be open to learning, Loving Lord, no matter my age or station in life.

Joy and Comfort, In Any Language

Kathy Lord and Susan Weber are professional performers who can perform in English, French, Greek, Hebrew, Italian, Russian or Spanish.

Their talents, however, are not typically featured on a grand stage or in a sold-out stadium. Their audience is usually children in hospital wards, homeless shelters, burn units or hospices.

Through a program called Music That Heals, Lord and Weber visit sick, homeless and dying children, as well as those with special needs, and bring the joy of uplifting music where it is needed most.

Lifting the spirits of those in distress is a form of love. Reach out to those afflicted in body, mind or spirit. Stay mindful of the healing power of positive, uplifting words and music.

David took the lyre and played it...and Saul would be relieved and feel better, and the evil spirit would depart from him. (1 Samuel 16:23)

Ease the suffering of little children, Divine Physician. May they find solace and joy through others' caring.

Beneath the Beach – History

Florida's Gulf Coast represents fun and frivolity to many. Dotted with burger joints and, especially during spring break, beach parties, the landscape belies its extraordinary archaeological treasures.

Archaeologists have discovered that by around 800 A.D., the Calusa people lived around the Gulf Coast in a politically complex society. Hereditary chiefs controlled the distribution of coastal resources.

The Calusa were skilled artisans, carving ceremonial wooden masks, among other items. More importantly, Calusa architecture, which included large causeways, canals, ramps and other shell and earthworks, likely served as the foundation for today's waterway system in many sections of the region.

A region's beginning may bear little resemblance to its present. How much do you know about your own beginnings? Ask relatives about your family's history. Gather oral stories, photographs or video clips. Your family's journey, like you, is unique.

You knit me together in my mother's womb. I praise You, for I am fearfully and wonderfully made. (Psalm 139:13-14)

Loving Creator, help me accept and love myself as You made me.

Do to others...

"If I ever have to be diapered and fed, I hope there will be someone kind enough to treat me with dignity and to see my humanity," says New York special ed teacher Ed Simon of East Harlem's P S 79. Daily, he and four paraprofessionals teach, feed and diaper 12 "SIE-1" or "12:1:4" pupils (12 pupils, 1 teacher, at least four paraprofessionals per class).

These high school students have profound cognitive impairments and medical conditions. Simon says, "They're a lot more aware than you think. ...It's a fatal assumption to think that they're not going to benefit."

With the insight of 27 years experience, Ed Simon adds, "These children have personalities, abilities, feelings, humanity...They are deserving of the respect and dignity that we (have). They may learn differently, but they can learn."

Do we treat young people and adults with serious challenges as we would want to be treated if we became impaired?

In everything do to others as you would have them do to you. (Matthew 7:12)

God, bless teachers and paraprofessionals who devote themselves to educating profoundly handicapped children.

Priceless Good Humor

In tough times, a sense of humor can be our saving grace.

Steve Rizzo, author of *Becoming a Humor Being,* recalls a TV interview that took place shortly after September 11, 2001. A firefighter, injured in the collapse of the World Trade Center, suffered a broken leg. A reporter asked, "How is it that you've come out of this alive?"

Without skipping a beat, he answered, "Look, lady, I'm from New York and I'm a firefighter; that's all you need to know."

Rizzo said, "Everyone laughed and though the laughter was only a couple of seconds, sometimes that's all you need to catch your second wind. ...If you can still laugh even a little amid the pain and chaos, you're going to be OK. ...We have to send a message that our spirit won't die. One important thing that unites us is our ability to laugh."

Share good cheer and laughter with those around you.

I commend enjoyment for there is nothing better for people...than to...enjoy themselves. (Ecclesiastes 8:15)

Help me enjoy a good laugh today, Spirit of Joy, and to share good humor and cheer with others.

Doorway to the Past

To listen to singer-songwriter Ani DiFranco talk about doors is almost a spiritual experience.

The celebrated performer, who is originally from Buffalo, New York, feels passionately about preserving her hometown's heritage. Besides working to preserve and restore some of the city's older buildings, she has made a 1910-built brick house there her home. To Ani DiFranco, the history of her new home holds near-sacred significance.

"Living in an old house now, opening my kitchen door with its old knob, touching it every day, I think of how many people over the past 100 years have walked through that doorway," she says. "I think about how I'm connected to things that came before me and to things that will come after me. That kind of experience reinforces my humanity."

Think about your connection to your ancestors and others who lived before you were born. Explore both your roots and history. Discover a fresh perspective on the world.

God spoke to our ancestors in many and various ways by the prophets, but in these last days He has spoken to us by a Son. (Hebrews 1:1-2)

Grant eternal rest to our ancestors, Just Judge.

On Behalf of Listeners

What did he say? What did she answer?

From discussions of intimate matters, to emotionally-charged outbursts, to gross obscenities, people seem to be using language that seems to bother listeners more than the speaker.

Because each one of us is a person of innate, God-given worth, that means our beliefs and their expression are of value, too. And so, those who hear what we have to say should be valued. When words pointlessly affront the feelings of listeners, it shows disrespect, even contempt.

We need to make an effort to see that our words reflect our best; that we are honest and truthful while showing the respect and love for others that God asks of us. We need to speak as we would be spoken to, because what we are really talking about is the Golden Rule.

And that's the true measure of everyone.

With (the tongue) we bless the Lord and Father, and with it we curse those who are made in the likeness of God. ...My brothers and sisters, this ought not to be so. (James 3:9-10)

I need to think before I speak, Spirit of Counsel. Remind me to honor myself and my listeners with my words.

The Duty of Peace

"Peace is not the product of terror or fear. Peace is not the silence of cemeteries. Peace is not the result of violent repression. Peace is the generous, tranquil contribution of all to the good of all. Peace is dynamism. Peace is generosity. It is right and it is duty."

Those are the words of Archbishop Oscar Romero of El Salvador. He was martyred in 1980 because he spoke out against the repression and brutality of his country's government, and on behalf of his people, who were poor and without power or hope.

Speaking to his people, Romero also said, "I want to be God's servant and yours. The prophetic mission is a duty of God's people. So, when I am told in a somewhat mocking tone that I think I am a prophet, I reply: 'God be praised! You ought to be one, too'."

We ought to be, indeed.

Whoever serves Me must follow Me, and where I am, there will My servant be also. Whoever serves Me, the Father will honor. (John 12:26)

The cost of peace is high, Prince of Peace. May I be willing to pay it for Your sake.

New Directions

When then 14-year-old and pregnant Judith Cunningham's guidance counselor asked her not to come back to school because she would "be a bad influence," she ended up on welfare in a roach-infested apartment.

Experiences like Cunningham's are why, in the late 1990s, Carolyn Anderson and Kathleen Cave began New Directions for Living, an organization that teaches troubled young women self-sufficiency. Searching for jobs, apartments and colleges are just a few of the ways in which New Directions aids them.

"When a client sees what their strengths are, what kind of things they bring to the table, they're elated," said Cunningham, who is now the Executive Director of New Directions.

Helping exploited women and girls discover their talents and gifts can give them happiness and a solid future. Find the good in those you know, and you will all be more fortunate for it.

A man who had died was...his mother's only son, and she was a widow...the Lord...had compassion for her. (Luke 7:12, 13)

Jesus, Son of Mary, how can we help Your most vulnerable children?

Still Praying

Day or night, one will always find at least two Franciscan Sisters of Perpetual Adoration at prayer in their La Crosse, Wisconsin chapel. In fact, for 125 years, since 11 a.m. on August 1, 1878, the Sisters have been praying before the Blessed Sacrament in shifts.

Praying for those who seek their intercession, they ask for God's help with everything from the safekeeping of soldiers and healing from cancer to job promotions and good test grades.

The Sisters say it is the nation's longest uninterrupted prayer, and the "perpetual adoration clock" is still ticking.

These Sisters remind us that God's "help line" is always open, that we can never run out of "anytime" minutes, and that we need to pray for others as well as ourselves.

With my voice I cry to the Lord; with my voice I make supplication to the Lord. I pour out my complaint before Him. (Psalm 142:1-2)

As often as I call upon You, Lord, hear my prayers.

The Soul of Lady Liberty

Emma Lazarus was born in 1849 to a prosperous New York City sugar merchant and his wife. The early writings of this author of the now-famous inscription on the Statue of Liberty were romantic poems. Ralph Waldo Emerson later became her mentor. "Write with passion," he told her.

That passion was awakened in Lazarus by a firsthand encounter with Jewish refugees who flooded into New York in the summer of 1881. One August morning, Lazarus went to visit these émigrés on Wards Island as part of a welfare committee. She saw the awful human conditions; heard stories of persecution and unimaginable hardships endured because of their religious beliefs. That experience inspired "The New Colossus," the inscription on the pedestal of the Statue of Liberty.

They include the words: "Give me your tired, your poor, your huddled masses yearning to breathe free..."

True communication always includes a meeting of minds–and hearts.

Proclaim liberty to the captives, and release to the prisoners. (Isaiah 61:1)

Give strength to the suffering, Master. May their burdens be lifted in Your compassion.

Knit One, Purl 200,000

In 1996, one of the editors of *Guideposts* wrote a short article about knitting sweaters for poor children.

Almost immediately, sweaters started arriving at the magazine's offices. Soon boxes of the woolen creations were stacked everywhere.

Guideposts contacted organizations such as Heart to Heart International and World Vision to get the sweaters where they were needed, distributing them from Bosnia to Rwanda, as well as here in the United States.

Every time the magazine published an article showing children from needy areas wrapped in the brightly colored garments, the editors braced for another avalanche of sweaters to show up in the mailroom. A box that arrived in the winter of 2003 pushed the total from the effort, now called "Knit for Kids," over the 200,000 mark.

Every little kindness we do in life adds up. And together, our actions can make a difference for a waiting, needy world.

As God's chosen ones...clothe yourselves with compassion, kindness, humility, meekness and patience. (Colossians 3:12)

Wrap me in Your love, Spirit of Compassion, so that we can face the rough times together.

Sharing Grief and Hope

When a 9-year-old Palestinian boy died in a car accident, his grief-stricken family wanted some good to come from their terrible loss. They offered his organs for transplants.

"For us, there is no difference between Jews and Arabs," said the boy's uncle, Jamil Salhuth. "We told the doctors that if there are patients who might be helped by his body parts, we agreed to it as an act of humanity."

And that's how Amin Salhuth saved the lives of five Israelis. His heart, lungs, liver and both kidneys were successfully transplanted into young people aged 6 to 29-years-old.

The loss of a loved one, especially a child, causes overwhelming grief. But knowing that good can be done to benefit the lives of others may provide some consolation.

Extend yourself to anyone suffering through bereavement. Be willing to share your time, to reach out—and to listen.

Blessed are those who mourn, for they will be comforted. (Matthew 5:4)

Loving God, help me open my heart to those who know the pain of loss. Help me be present to those in grief.

Leaving a Career, Getting Class

Janice Crowley made good money as a phone-system salesperson in Wichita, Kansas. But something was missing, so she went looking for answers—finding them in a classroom.

Although her pay these days is one-fourth what her former sales career offered, the city's teens are far richer since Crowley switched to teaching chemistry at Wichita Collegiate School.

In the past 20 years, she's trained many young scientists, including some whose research has been featured in news articles and scientific journals.

Students cherish Crowley for taking chemistry out of textbooks. "Kids want to hear the stories first," she says. "Then you rope them in."

For example, in her classroom, Crowley explains acid-base properties to students by having dentists tell them what bulimia does to teeth.

When deciding what to do in life, it's possible to make a change for yourself—and then make a real difference for others.

A disciple is not above the teacher, but everyone who is fully qualified will be like the teacher. (Luke 6:40)

Help me learn Your ways, Divine Master, so that I may serve You in those in need.

Shed One Tear

World War II was being waged. Keijiro Matsushima was six-years old when, on August 6, 1945 his hometown of Hiroshima, Japan was the target for the world's first atomic bomb.

Matsushima remembers sitting in his math class when the bomb exploded. He was wounded by flying glass, and he remembers thinking at that moment, that he was going to die. Then, all of a sudden, everything went eerily silent.

Because everything was destroyed around him, the little boy was forced to walk home, past the destruction and countless dead bodies. He reached home at midnight.

Today, at 75, Keijiro travels the world, telling his story and encouraging nations to end nuclear weapons testing. He says, "Shed one tear for the victims of Hiroshima, and then think of tomorrow. Never use (nuclear bombs) again."

Practice peace in your daily dealings with others. Do what you can to promote peace on a global basis.

If you love those who love you, what credit is that to you?...Love your enemies. ...Be merciful. (Luke 6:32,35,36)

Holy Trinity, inspire us to resolve our differences peacefully.

Develop Self-Discipline

Part of true maturity is learning self-discipline.

John MacArthur, writing in *The Pillars of Christian Character*, offers these ideas on helping ourselves:

- Start with small things.
- Get yourself organized.
- Don't constantly seek to be entertained.
- Be on time.
- Keep your word.
- Do the most difficult tasks first.
- Finish what you start.
- Accept correction.
- Practice self-denial.
- Welcome responsibility.

Only if we can control ourselves in small matters will we ever be able to do so in important circumstances. Love yourself—and that means doing what is good and right, not just comfortable.

The wise of heart is called perceptive. (Proverbs 16:21)

Spirit of Light, illuminate my path and strengthen my resolve to do Your will.

Latte Love Affair

When Angelo Giuliano moved to Boulder, Colorado, he quickly established a morning routine: hit the gym, swing by Starbucks, and then head for work.

In her 20s like Angelo and also new in town, Leah Mazur had taken a part-time job, but made a stop at Starbucks a priority before beginning her workday.

"I had a crush on him the second he walked through the door," says Leah. Angelo was likewise in love but it took him several weeks before he gave Leah his telephone number.

Their first date included a shared potent chai latte. And their courtship, once started, was a whirlwind of romance. Eight months after that first date, Angelo proposed. Appropriately, it was during a morning get-together right there in Starbucks. And when Angelo asked, Leah said, "Yes," even before he had finished the question.

Love can find you anywhere. All that's needed is an open mind and heart.

Love is strong as death, passion fierce as the grave. ...Many waters cannot quench love, neither can floods drown it. (Song of Solomon 8:6,7)

Father, when I am lonely or afraid, send Your Spirit to comfort and calm me.

Camp Lessons for City and Country Kids

While visiting the rugged Sharpe Reservation in upstate New York as part of the annual Fresh Air Fund program, a group of nine-year-old girls had their assumptions about pigs challenged.

"Pigs are one of the cleanest animals," said one of the camp staff while the girls standing at the pigpen had a chance to pet the squealing creatures.

Each summer thousands of young "city slickers" become "country bumpkins" by participating in the special summer program. These excursions where urban youth meet their rural counterparts have a way of shattering other stereotypes as well. Whether they're used to cement sidewalks or wide-open farmland, these children learn more about what they have in common than what divides them. And everyone has fun in the process.

Whatever promotes mutual understanding and respect is vitally important.

Agree with one another, live in peace.
(2 Corinthians 13:11)

Remind us, Lord, of Creation's healing, calming presence.

A Good Gig

As a University of North Carolina student in the 1980s, Tim Duffy decided to preserve the sounds of the mountain musicians all around him.

Duffy recorded unheralded blues music and also noticed the musicians' poverty. Even if taped and archived, "the recordings don't put food on their table; it doesn't get them a gig."

According to a *New York Times* story, Duffy and his wife Denise began the Music Maker Foundation, a nonprofit organization, which assists artists.

Elderly and infirm musicians can get cash for groceries or emergencies. Formerly unknown performers tour the U.S. and Europe, sell CDs, and find respect for their talent.

"Sometimes people stop me on the street and say, 'Aren't you famous?'" said John Dee Holman. "Now that's real nice," said the musician who spent much of his life as a heavy machine operator.

Respect people's talents, whatever they are.

**Wine and music gladden the heart.
(Sirach 40:20)**

Inspire musicians, Holy Spirit. Help them use their gifts well.

Rituals and Routines

Family routines and rituals can be good for physical and mental well-being.

In a study in *The Journal of Family Psychology,* Dr. Barbara H. Fiese of Syracuse University found that routines are "settled patterns of activity or communication" and that rituals "evoked emotions or conferred meaning."

Fiese notes, "If you don't think about it after it's over or wouldn't miss it, it's a routine." Fiese found routines appear to have benefits in terms of physical health or emotional well-being.

Children in families with predicable routines had better overall health. Rituals have a greater effect on emotional health. In families with rituals, teens have a stronger sense of self, couples report happier marriages, and children have greater interaction with grandparents.

Fiese advises: "Sit down as a family and try to figure out three things everybody looks forward to, and try to preserve them."

Celebrate your family in ways large and small.

Celebrate your festivals! (Nahum 1:15)

Remind parents to establish and maintain their family's religious and secular rituals, Loving Lord.

Does Nursing Need Critical Care?

"Many unexpected health crises occur not when technology fails but when a patient's condition changes and no one notices," writes Cornelia Dean in *The New York Times*.

Nurses are the traditional specialists in bedside care, trained to observe and respond when a patient is in medical distress. But in her review of Suzane Gordon's book, *Nursing Against the Odds: How Health Care Cost Cutting, Media Stereotypes and Medical Hubris Undermine Nurses and Patient Care*, Dean writes that Gordon provides a gloomy assessment of the nursing field today.

Many nurses face mandatory overtime, the stress of looking after patients often in need of high tech intervention, and the demands of intense physical labor. Managed care has also been hard on nurses when hospital budgets need cutting. More than that, there are continuing issues of respect – or its lack – that keep nurses from feeling valued as key members of the medical field.

Offer respect and appreciation to everyone you meet.

Judge with right judgment. (John 7:24)

Bless nurses, Merciful Savior.

Art: A World of Wonder

Creating art is "more about leaping than knowing how you will land," says Laura Baring-Gould. Her art has been described as using familiar forms and daring exploration to nudge us out of routine perceptions.

"My work, at its core," says Baring-Gould "is about the way that we all need to be reminded of possibility and wonder....to (help) people... understand their relationships with each other, with their physical surroundings, and with their capacity to imagine and create." She feels we all hunger to be part of a community.

One observer of Baring-Gould exhibits says people come in groups, "sometimes meditation groups, sometimes they're just kids, but when they enter into Laura's created spaces they somehow are transformed by the art. She's a master at creating space in which people can become their most authentic selves."

Whatever it takes, be your most authentic self.

You shall love your neighbor as yourself. (Mark 12:31)

Abba, remind us that we can not love anyone if we do not first have a healthy love for ourselves, "as is," warts and all.

A Man of Vision

"It was always the warrior's role to protect his people," said Dennis Hastings, chief of the Omahas. "I'm always asking myself what can I do to protect the tribe."

Hastings' mission has become that of recovering the Omaha's culture. People suffer when they are estranged from their own history, Hastings believes. And too often the Omahas feel like strangers in their ancestral land, according to an article in *My Generation*.

When Hastings was first involved in this work, he became angry at the problems facing the Omaha tribe: "Alcoholism, unemployment, welfare dependency and shattered families."

Nevertheless, Hastings wants to help his people one step at a time. "If you can get each person to be proud of himself, then, little by little, you can get the whole tribe to become proud."

One day, Hastings wants all his people to say and really feel "My people matter!"

Let's remember that all people matter.

There was a great multitude...from every nation, from all tribes and peoples and languages, standing before the throne and before the Lamb. (Revelation 7:9)

Forgive us, Creator, for our sins against one another.

To Be Holy

Who are the everyday saints you know?

They may not be performing miracles on street corners, but they are surely developing a deep relationship with God and reaching out to others because of the faith, hope and love which are at the center of their lives.

"There is only one way to love God and to prove it to Him, and that is by loving your neighbor—the person next to you at any given moment,' wrote Catherine Doherty, founder of Madonna House, and a woman of great courage and commitment to the poor.

"Turning your face and heart to Christ simply means turning your face to the one who is next to you at this moment in your life. If you do that, dearly beloved, you shall become a saint."

Seek God's will; do good for His children.

The good person brings good things out of a good treasure. (Matthew 12:35).

Help me to see Your face when I turn to my neighbor, Holy Jesus.

Finding Joy in Nature

As the mother of young children, writer Julie Clark Robinson thought she just needed some adult conversation. But she discovered she actually wanted something else.

"I tried the walk-with-a-girlfriend thing. It's a good way to get the exercise, have a great gabfest. But it didn't work for me because I realized that what I really wanted was quiet."

Quieting ourselves isn't always easy. "The first few blocks or so, I can't help but think such profound thoughts as 'If I hurry and fold the laundry, then put the roast in, I can take a shower before dark'."

But appreciating nature is joyful. "For me, walking isn't about getting back into my old jeans after having two babies in three years," writes Robinson. "Walking is about taking a mental break."

Isn't it time for a restorative walk of your own?

(Jesus) said to them, "Come away to a deserted place all by yourselves and rest a while." (Mark 6:31)

May the works of Your hands soothe my stress-frazzled body, mind and soul, Divine Physician.

A Better Way to Criticize

If you hate to be criticized, you're not alone. Even on those occasions when its really necessary, criticism is often given in such a negative way that we feel offended.

Neil Eskelin, writing in *Leading with Love,* offers these principles of positive criticism:

- Never point out errors without offering a solution. The time for correction must also become a time to teach.
- Criticize the act, never the person. Why deflate someone's ego when your goal is to improve performance? People have emotions that need to be respected.
- Never scold in public. Even if the error is minor, don't embarrass someone by pointing out mistakes in front of colleagues.
- Always end with praise. While some believe you should start with a compliment and end with correction, it's better to end on a positive note.

And always put yourself in the other person's place. Criticize the way you would want someone to criticize you.

Judge your neighbor's feelings by your own, and in every matter be thoughtful. (Sirach 31:15)

Jesus, let me never use my words to inflict pain on others.

A Driving Force

It's amazing how our lives have changed since the invention of the automobile.

Decades after its initial 1908 introduction, the famous Model T automobile is back. Ford Motor Company commissioned a few of these legendary vehicles in time for the company's centennial celebrations.

At one time, early in the 1900s, half of the cars on Earth were Model Ts. Actually the Model T never completely left the road. Thousands are said to still be out there in running condition.

The automobile has had a profound effect on our world, locally and globally. And as is the case with most technology, it has been a mixed blessing.

If we're wise, we will keep this in mind as the next new thing comes along.

The discerning person looks to wisdom. (Proverbs 17:24)

Holy Spirit, give us wisdom.

Hope Builders

If they wrote about "how they spent their summer vacation," a group of Muncie, Indiana, youth would include the following: painting, weeding, cooking and building.

The program, "Building the City of God," is sponsored by three Catholic parishes in the area, St. Mary, St. Francis of Assisi and St. Lawrence.

"I love to work with wood and I love to dig," said Megan Burkhardt.

She and three other young people helped to build a wheelchair ramp for one area resident.

Mothers and fathers also joined in. "My family likes this type of work," said the mother of Aaron Gordon who was also involved in the ramp project.

"I'm so grateful for the work that was done," said one beneficiary of their summertime efforts. "It's beautiful. I know this is an answer to a prayer."

The good that we do – alone or with others – can bring joy to others and satisfy our souls.

God...will not overlook your work and the love that you showed for His sake. (Hebrews 6:10)

We are Your children, Father, and we hunger for Your love.

She Let the Dogs In

Special education teacher Jennifer Wise, known for her innovative teaching of emotionally handicapped children, was the choice for a new program to help lead troubled teens to a better future – by letting the dogs in!

"Kids and Canines" at Tampa's Dorothy Thomas Exceptional Center, is a place for chronic truants and other teens who can't seem to get along at traditional schools. The teens spend part of each day training and caring for service dogs.

Some 60 young people have benefited. Kari Tolbert refused to go to school for a year until she was placed in the program. "I hated being around a lot of people," she explained. "I had bad anxiety. But being with the dogs and going out in public helped a lot. I've learned patience – and responsibility."

Sometimes, with the right approach, you can teach someone a new and improved way of life.

All His creatures do His will. (Sirach 42:15)

Thank You, Blessed Trinity, for the healing, companionship and wisdom dogs, cats and other creatures can give us.

Enjoying Classical Music

Jennifer Higdon, a 40-something contemporary composer whose early influences, besides her parents, were the Beatles and her high school marching band, trained at Philadelphia's Curtis Institute of Music.

She is considered one of our best classical composers, according to *Body & Soul* magazine. As an article says, Higdon's music is "a lot of fun to listen to, and audiences–regular people–just love her stuff."

Higdon says, "Composing's just putting sounds together. I think most people compose all the time; they just don't know it. It's just like banging on pots and pans when you were little."

Some think classical music is just for academic "stuffed shirts" and aficionados interested in mathematically precise, but popularly inaccessible, works.

Be informed. Then judge for yourself.

Do not judge by appearances, but judge with right judgment. (John 7:24)

Remind me, Holy Spirit, to think for myself, to exercise those critical faculties and the intelligence You have given me.

The Fight for Civil Rights

Long before he was elected to Congress, John Lewis was arrested 40 times, beaten unconscious and had his skull fractured by a law-enforcement officer while on a non-violent civil rights march in Alabama.

Lewis' life was in danger and he felt fear, yet he continued to struggle for equal rights under the law.

"You cannot be preoccupied by fear," said Lewis. "I think you have what I call 'an executive decision' with yourself. You say, 'I am not going to be afraid: I am going to go on.'

"You come to that point where you think that something is so right, so necessary, so good to be doing that you have to do it, so you overcome the fear of being hurt or even killed."

In every day and age there comes a decisive moment when citizens have to acknowledge the injustice in their midst. And then they must act.

I am laying in Zion a foundation stone...and I will make justice the line, and righteousness the plummet. (Isaiah 28:16,17)

May justice and righteousness be the measure of our lives, Mighty One of Jacob!

Apron Memories

Memory is a strange and wonderful thing.

EllyAnne Geisel plumbed its depths when she created "The Apron Chronicles," an art exhibit. For a few years, she carried around a laundry basket of old aprons which complete strangers were invited to touch and talk about.

The aprons elicited strong emotions.

For Mimi Harrison, writing in *Time* magazine, aprons, like baby blankets are "rich with sentiment and associations. Store-bought or homemade, flower print or flour sack, an apron does double duty as protection and decoration." Aprons also evoke domesticity.

Aprons reminded one 13-year-old of the grandmother with whom she sews and bakes.

What memories move you?

The memory of the righteous is a blessing. (Proverbs 10:7)

Bless women and girls, Creator.

A Horse of a Different Finish

In 1994 jockey Mike Smith rode the favorite, Holy Bull, in the Kentucky Derby. The horse finished 12th, beating just two other horses.

Eleven years later, Smith once again found himself aboard a Derby contender–Giacomo–a son, in fact, of that 1994 ill-fated finisher, and a horse whose odds were set at 50 to one.

"The first time I got on this horse, before he ever ran, I said this horse was going to redeem his father's name," Smith said. Giacomo did just that, defying the odds and winning the 2005 Kentucky Derby.

A jockey who has ridden other Derby favorites, and even finished second in two such horse races, Smith began to wonder if he would ever add a win to his resume. "It pays to hang in there," he advised.

In life, too, whether a long shot or a sure thing, it always pays to do your best–and hang on until the finish line.

Bear fruit with patient endurance. (Luke 8:15)

Lord, sustain me in the trials of this day, knowing that win or lose, Your love is a sure thing.

Pulling Life's Emergency Cord

Ann's life was filling up fast. A full-time, pressure-packed weekday job, plus nights and weekends as a waitress/manager at her husband's café left little time for Ann—let alone for her six-year-old Hannah.

When her daughter asked to speak with her through the bathroom door one evening, Ann decided to make a change. "I was on a runaway train going wherever it went," she said. "I decided to chart a few stops for myself."

First, Ann hired someone to work Friday evenings at the café. Then she called a "meeting" with Hannah. "Friday nights are ours," she told her, "for dinner and for whatever we want to do."

So far mom and daughter have taken in a community theater play, rented movies, gone shopping, and simply walked and talked *together*.

In life, the "doing" isn't as important as the "being" there for the people you love.

Love one another deeply from the heart.
(1 Peter 1:22)

Slow me down, today, Master, so that I might not miss any experience of You.

Leaving a Legacy

Born in the early 1920's, Robert Blackburn was the founder of the influential Printmaking Workshop. In its obituary, the *New York Times* said the workshop "assumed a catalytic role in the 'print boom' of the '60s, but never lost its communal flavor. Anyone could walk in and use the presses, inks and papers" for a nominal fee.

"Mr. Blackburn and a series of assistants instructed fledgling printmakers in basic techniques and worked with experienced artists on complicated projects."

Blackburn, who learned printmaking at the Art Students League during the Depression, had been assured by his lithography teacher, Will Barnet, that printmaking "was a primary art form worth focusing on as a career."

Now, there are plans to have the Library of Congress acquire the Workshop's 12,000 prints.

What will be your legacy? How will you assure its survival?

In Christ we have also obtained an inheritance. (Ephesians 1:11)

Thank You, Messiah, for the inheritance You have bought for us. May the way we live our lives reflect our gratitude.

Hair Doctors

In one Texas barbershop you can "take a little off on the sides" and check your blood pressure. And if your pressure shows warning signs, the barber will refer you to medical help.

Likewise at a beauty shop in Alabama. There, stylists were trained to talk to clients about breast and cervical cancer. Pamphlets are also available. One year after those discussions started, 69 percent of customers either had or planned to have a mammogram; 94 percent had already had a Pap smear or planned to have one soon.

Bringing health education to the comfort of barbershops and beauty salons is the result of research programs developed at UT Southwestern Medical Center in Dallas and at the University of Alabama at Birmingham.

So the next time you tend to how you look on the outside, make sure you care for your inner workings, as well. It's even more important to be healthy than to look good.

Health and fitness are better than any gold, and a robust body than countless riches. There is no wealth better than health of body. (Sirach 30:15-16)

Send Your healing to me and those whom I love, Divine Physician.

Scientific Study of Religious Experience

The Gallup Institute's mission "is to discover and implement new ideas for society in the areas of education, environment, health, religion and values," according to George Gallup, Jr.

"We seek to showcase ideas to move society in a more positive direction, conduct surveys on these, and present these to leaders who can disseminate the information."

Gallup finds that there is a growing interest in spirituality. He speculates that people are yearning for more meaningful relationships with one another. Gallup says that, until recently, prayer's impact had not been explored.

He continues, "only near the end of the 20th century" did we start "paying attention to the spiritual life."

For some, scientific exploration into prayer, meditation and spirituality is important. For others, prayer, meditation and spirituality themselves are all that's important.

What's important is to open yourself to God.

Whenever you pray, go into your room and shut the door and pray to your Father who is in secret; and your Father who sees in secret will reward you. (Matthew 6:6)

Father, teach me to love spontaneous prayer.

Learning the Ways of the World

Software giant Microsoft learned an extremely valuable lesson: cross-cultural ignorance can be costly and offensive.

Microsoft developers had used a color on a map of India to signify the disputed territory of Kashmir. When that software was distributed which showed Kashmir separate from India not only were Indian governmental officials insulted, but they banned Microsoft Word from their country. The company had to revise the software to the tune of hundreds of thousands of dollars.

Keep in mind that:

- Jokes rarely translate well across cultural lines.
- In some Asian countries, avoiding eye contact is considered respectful.
- In the Middle East, it's an insult to show the sole of your shoe.
- Many cultures observe strict protocols for seating arrangements, menu choices and the presence of alcohol.

Variety, awareness and especially respect make the world go 'round–smoothly.

Conduct yourselves honorably. (1 Peter 2:12)

Lord, instill in me a respect for all cultures and traditions.

Not Taking 'No' for an Answer

When Cheryl Sudduth first started working for Calidad Industries, a company that places disabled workers in government-agency jobs, she heard the word "no" a lot.

It was a disturbing trend for the Californian who emphasizes her aversion to taking "no" for an answer. To counter objections from the agencies to such placements, Sudduth decided to change the way people looked at persons with disabilities.

She spoke to experts on the subject, educating herself. Then she lobbied for a training program to teach managers how to work with disabled people. Finally she brought in volunteers. The tide soon changed—with a dramatic increase in new hires who were disabled.

"I want to shift our culture's focus away from surface things and bring out the essence of people," Sudduth explains. "I want my children to understand that we all have disabilities. Some are just visible."

Don't let prejudice influence the way you see others.

You shall not revile the deaf or put a stumbling block before the blind; you shall fear your God; I am the Lord. (Leviticus 19:14)

Lord, enable me to see the real beauty in people.

Rewriting Your Prayer Plan

Ever "hit a wall" spiritually? Sometimes, no matter how hard we pray for something, it just doesn't seem to happen. Or, we find ourselves with little will or incentive to keep praying.

When writer Karen Barber experienced this, she wrote an article in *Guideposts* magazine in which she asks, "Could it be that our prayers are sometimes answered more fully than we sometimes realize?

Barber reaches a thought-provoking conclusion: "Maybe it's not that there aren't answers to each and every one of our prayers. It's that we don't know where or how to look for them."

Berber began keeping a prayer log, and learned that sometimes, the answers to her prayers were right in front of her. It was up to her to make the time and have the serenity to learn how to recognize them.

Learn to pray from the heart. Then keep alert for the answers.

Lord, teach us to pray..."When you pray, say, Father, hallowed be Your Name." (Luke 11:1,2)

Jesus, teach me to pray in my own words and with an open heart.

Stained Glass Lessons

Stained glass began in the 11th century and apparently so did its dual function as adornment and means of instruction.

At St. Catherine's School in Richmond, Virginia, a girls' school, students see the young Catherine not only defending Christianity against pagan philosophers but converting them, too.

In a window at the Beauvoir School at the National Cathedral in Washington, students see third-grade teacher Julia Morse helping a child focus a telescope on the stars.

Finally in the stained glass windows in the Benevolent Chapel in Brooklandville, Maryland, students see, among others, Hilda of Whitby, Sojourner Truth and Eleanor Buchanan Rogers, who, in 1799, helped found the Benevolent orphanage and school itself.

Whether stained glass windows, books or any other source, children need good role models to make the most of their lives.

Train children in the right way, and when old they will not stray. (Proverbs 22:6)

Inspire all adults to be sound role models for children and youth, Jesus of Nazareth.

Gladly Going Back to the Drawing Board

When a sinus infection led to a spinal cord infection, New Jersey architect and designer Michael Graves was paralyzed from the waist down

"Right after it happened," Graves recalls, "I said, 'Why me?' But soon I realized that you have to forget that, because who knows why you or me—it's not going to change."

And so the architect, who designed Walt Disney Company headquarters in Burbank, California, the new U.S. Embassy complex in Seoul, Korea, and the O'Reilly Theater in Pittsburgh, decided to go back to the drawing board. He began reviewing projects and meeting with associates while still in rehabilitation.

Physical therapy continues, but the prospects of walking again remain uncertain for the septuagenarian. What is certain is a new focus—making his buildings more accessible to disabled persons.

Remember, every life event challenges our strengths and strengthens our potential for growth.

As he was...approaching Damascus, suddenly a light from heaven flashed around him. He fell to the ground and heard a voice saying to him, "Saul, Saul, why do you persecute Me?" (Acts 9:3-4)

When I feel most alone, Lord, guide me.

Delay a Good Thing

A group of Catholic journalists from the United States were to make a pilgrimage and study tour of Poland in the spring of 2005. Twice the trip was delayed by the Polish government, moving the departure from mid-March to the first Saturday in April.

As the group of 15 writers, editors and photographers boarded the plane on April 2, Pope John Paul II, Karol Jozef Wotyla died. Suddenly the trip became the journalism experience of a lifetime, with a wealth of story and photo opportunities and a firsthand experience of that pope's influence on his homeland.

One editor said, "We were working day and night—and we were exhausted. But nothing will ever take away what we saw and heard in that week."

Sometimes the clouds that gather in our lives can, in an instant, break apart for the sunshine.

The Lord is my shepherd, I shall not want. He makes me lie down in green pastures; He leads me beside still waters...He leads me in right paths for His name's sake. (Psalm 23:1-2,3)

Help me see Your hand in all things, Lord. Grant me always Your peace.

Illustrating Leadership

Fans of the cartoon *Dilbert* appreciate Scott Adams' caustic take on the daily frustrations of business.

It was, in fact, those same frustrations that led to Adams' cartoonist career. After 17 years at an unrewarding middle-management job, he decided to make a move. But before he became a leader in his field, Adams made sure he was building success with a positive attitude and businesslike methods such as:

Affirmation. He wrote out "I will become a syndicated cartoonist" 15 times a day.

Persistence. Despite rejections–many of them–he kept sending sample cartoons to syndication services.

Customer focus. When he did land a syndicated contract, he started talking to readers who told him that business humor was the next popular trend. Adams refocused his work–and the rest is comic strip history.

No matter our chosen path in life, it is best trod with a professional and positive outlook.

Are not two sparrows sold for a penny? Yet not one of them will fall to the ground apart from Your Father...you are of more value than many sparrows. (Matthew 10:29,30)

Help me have faith in myself, Holy God.

Beauty–Inside Out

Inner beauty is in. That's the message of *New Moon*, the magazine for and by "tween" girls–those who are in between being a young child and teenager.

The magazine's "Turn Beauty Inside Out" (TBIO) campaign helps girls define themselves from the inside out rather than by appearances, says Caroline Ticarro-Parker, executive director of Mind on the Media, a nonprofit group coordinating that effort.

Since 2001, *New Moon* has published a special "25 Beautiful Girls" issue, spotlighting inner beauty, and sponsored a TBIO Day. The message is a challenging one. Today, girls are more body conscious at an earlier age. In fact, one disturbing statistic indicates that the number of girls under the age of 18 who got breast implants increased from 3,872 in 2002 to 4,211 in 2004.

The ideal beauty? According to *New Moon's* editors it is someone who stands up for what is right. And that defines "beautiful" at every age.

Charm is deceitful, and beauty is vain, but a woman who fears the Lord is to be praised. (Proverbs 31:30)

Master, I long to do Your will.

Register and Vote

In the presidential election year 2000, only 60 percent of eligible voters in the United States registered, and of that number only 86 percent (that's 51.6 percent of eligible voters) actually went to the polls.

Elections are our opportunity to hire the people who run our local, state and federal governments. There is too much at stake to excuse anyone's absence.

If you are a regular voter, keep it up. If you need to register, do it. Your local library and the Web offer resources. And when you get it, share the information with others.

It isn't enough to have an opinion. Citizens need to back up their beliefs with a thoughtful decision in a voting booth.

James Madison, fourth U. S. president and known as the Father of the Constitution, said, "We have staked the whole future of America, not on the power of government–far from it–but on the capacity of mankind for self-government."

Proclaim liberty throughout the land to all its inhabitants. (Leviticus 25:10)

Holy Spirit, bless the people of this and every nation. And help us to be bearers of Your blessings to one another.

Getting More Than They Give

Volunteerism in the U.S. seems alive and well. According to a Bureau of Labor Statistics survey, about 59 million people volunteered at some point between September 2001 and September 2002.

The survey also found that slightly more than one in four persons aged 16 or older performed volunteer service. Yet, no matter their age, most of the volunteers said that in volunteering they receive more than they give.

It is truly in giving that we receive, sometimes much more than we ever expected. When individuals follow the example of Jesus, the world truly becomes a better place. What can you do today to feed the hungry, welcome a stranger and care for the sick?

If you have some time and a sense of commitment, seek out volunteer opportunities in your neighborhood.

A good measure, pressed down, shaken together, running over, will be put into your lap; for the measure you give will be the measure you get back. (Luke 6:38)

God, grant me a generous spirit so that I may better assist those who are less fortunate than I.

Raising Cheerful Givers

Dan Kindlon, author of *Too Much of a Good Thing,* feels that "kids need limits and responsibilities." He believes, that parents need to help their children develop a "giving" attitude.

Here are a few thoughts on accomplishing just that.

Chores. Having jobs around the house helps teach social responsibility.

Charity. Even a young child can set aside a small portion of his or her allowance for worthy causes.

Service. From food drives to park clean-ups, such activities emphasize that children are part of a larger family.

Happiness. Success is fine, but children need to know the greater value of being happy.

Spirituality. End the focus on "stuff" and begin to focus on relationships–with each other and with God.

God, our Father, gives us all good things. Parents need to focus less on the material and more on the soul and mind.

**A wise child makes a glad father.
(Proverbs 15:20)**

Show me the way to serve You, Lord, in today's details.

Catching the Word Thieves

Sometimes, when reading students' papers, Gillian Silverman's breathing quickens and her heart skips a beat because she detects the "purloining of ideas or language from another source"–plagiarism.

"It is literary theft," explains the usually mild-mannered English professor. "A plagiarized paper presents itself as an act of aggression, a taunt behind the title page."

When Silverman suspects plagiarism, she first browses the Web, a tool, she says, that has done much to accommodate such paper pilfering, for the source of the stolen material.

While she has empathy for her students, most of whom are working 12-hour night shifts to pay for college, she realizes that not revealing the plagiarizers would rob those students of the opportunity for an honest education.

One of the few things you can and should copy is honest behavior.

But as for that in the good soil, these are the ones who, when they hear the word, hold it fast in an honest and good heart, and bear fruit with patient endurance. (Luke 8:15)

Thank You, Father, for the unique gifts You have given me. Let me praise You by using them wisely, honestly.

Cheering on the Runners

Doctors at Maryland's Bethesda Naval Hospital had to amputate Lance Corporal Jeffrey Sanders' left leg above the knee. Sanders had been severely injured in a roadside explosion in a town south of Baghdad, Iraq.

Less than three months after being fitted with a prosthetic leg, Sanders, coached and encouraged by gold-medal paralympian "professionals" Dennis Oehler and Todd Schaffhauser, was running. He was part of a running clinic at a Maryland rehabilitation hospital led by Oehler and Schaffhauser. Some 40 amputees, including about a dozen veterans from Afghanistan and Iraq, attended.

"They prove that if you set your goals higher, it can be done," said Sanders about the two medalists. Sanders' goal: "to get back to where I was before Iskandariyah," the town where the blast occurred.

It is difficult to walk away from life's challenges, but hope-filled determination will always help.

All the boots of the tramping warriors and all the garments rolled in blood shall be burned...For a child has been born for us...named...Prince of Peace. (Isaiah 9:5,6)

When I feel defeated, send Your Spirit to lift me up, Jesus.

Prayers of Peace

When the World Trade Center collapsed after a terrorist attack, St. Paul's Episcopal Chapel became a haven for rescue workers as well as those who came to pay their respects to the dead.

The parishioners of St. Paul's chapel encourage all who come to pray for peace. These are among the prayers they share:

"Come let us go up to the mountain of the Lord, that we may walk the paths of the Most High. And we shall beat our swords into plowshare, and our spears into pruning hooks." (Judaism)

"Praise be to the Lord of the Universe who has created us and made us into tribes and nations that we may know each other, not that we may despise each other." (Islam)

"Blessed are the peacemakers, for they shall be known as the Children of God. ...Love your enemies, do good to those who hate you. ...And as you wish that others would do to you, do so to them." (Christianity)

In days to come...nation shall not lift up sword against nation, neither shall they learn war any more. (Isaiah 2:1,4)

Lord of all nations, help us to love one another.

Holding Love in the Palm of Your Hand

The first few weeks of first grade were tough on Elizabeth and her parents. Each morning, mother and father would walk her to school near their Bronx, New York, home and leave her there, crying inconsolably.

Then one Monday, on the walk, Elizabeth asked her mother and father to kiss the palm of each of her hands. That day and each day that week she made the same request. Suddenly, there were no tears when they left her at school, only smiles.

"What was that all about?" Elizabeth's mom finally asked her daughter.

"My teacher told me to do it," she explained about the hand-kissing. "I cry because I miss you. But now when I feel like crying, I press my hands to my face and it's like you and dad are there, kissing me. Then I'm not afraid and I don't cry."

Love comforts and strengthens the heart of the beloved.

Little children, let us love, not in word or speech, but in truth and action. (1 John 3:18)

Surround me with Your love, especially when I am alone and afraid, Abba.

From Soap Operas to the Priesthood

When Scott Binet was growing up, he was always fascinated with the Gospel stories about Jesus healing the sick. He felt the Lord calling him – but to what service?

After college, he landed some soap opera roles, but soon opted out of acting and enrolled in medical school.

When he treated a pregnant woman in asthmatic crisis who lost her child, he asked himself, "How do I want this patient – any patient – to see me?" "As Christ," was the answer – and he realized that he felt called to the priesthood.

Binet searched for a way to be both priest and doctor. Eventually, he connected with the Order of St. Camillus, a group of priests and religious brothers who care for the sick.

He had found the answer to his question, "What service?"

Our search for how God wants us to live our lives can be very complex, but eventually God will show us His way.

Be on your guard against all kinds of greed; for one's life does not consist in the abundance of possessions. (Luke 12:15)

Instruct me in the way I should walk, Lord. And remind me to travel light.

The American Dream

Queensborough Community College, like many community colleges, is home to ambitious men and women who dream, strive, and ultimately achieve.

Students face major challenges on their way to obtaining an academic degree and their own version of the American Dream.

Despite having cerebral palsy and using a wheelchair, Tommy Ge writes and performs in plays while completing an associate degree in fine and performing arts.

Marcella Powell detoured off the traditional educational path but got back on at Queensborough. After earning a GED diploma, she worked in the restaurant business. Now she's devoting time to studies in molecular biology. An honor student, she plans to go on for a master's and Ph.D. in the State University system.

Given others' support, persistence and hard work, people of all ages find that it's never too late to achieve major goals.

Support such people. (3 John 8)

Inspire many to rise above early limitations to achieve their full potential, Holy Spirit.

A Pharmacy for the Poor

The problem: Finding cures for the diseases of poverty which kill millions worldwide, but which get little attention from big drug companies, because even promising treatments won't be profitable.

The problem solver: Victoria Hale and the Institute for OneWorld Health (IOWH), America's first nonprofit pharmaceutical company.

Pharmaceutical companies donate patents from compounds they aren't using. Then with donor support, IOWH develops the compounds into drugs for diseases found in developing countries. The first, scheduled for approval in India in the fall of 2005, will treat a parasitic disease that kills 200,000 people a year.

Down the road IOWH is looking at drugs for malaria and diarrhea. Generous groups are starting to offer more patents, but, Hale says, "we only want to accept what we can develop."

Finding cures, like finding solutions, often just requires pointing minds and hearts in the right direction.

Blessed are those who trust in the Lord, whose trust is the Lord. They shall be like a tree planted by water. (Jeremiah 17:7-8)

I place my trust in You, Lord. You, are my hope.

Building Blocks Every Child Needs

From the moment a child is born, so is his self-esteem. Every time his mother or father looks down and says, "Aren't you wonderful?" the baby's heart rate speeds up; eyes widen and become bright. That body language proves the newborn understands that someone loves him passionately.

Unconditional love is the first building block of a child's self-esteem. Another is achievement, mastering tasks, even when failing at first. Through self-discipline, a child learns to stop himself or herself from losing control, thus feeling secure and confident. How else can parents help build self-esteem?

Accept each child's temperament as it is.

Comment on the things your children can do, not the ones they can't.

Praise them for their passion.

Be there for them when they are under stress and when decision-making feels overwhelming.

Build your child up, one hug at a time.

It was I who taught Ephraim to walk, I took them up in My arms...I was...who lift infants to their cheeks. I bent down to them and fed them. (Hosea 11:3,4)

We, Your children, praise You, Heavenly Father.

The Wilderness of Jersey City

When Steve Latham first began exploring the land along the abandoned reservoir in the Jersey City Heights area of New Jersey, it was strictly as a place to kayak and teach his kids about nature.

Slowly the exploration of the 14-plus acres turned into something between a cause and an obsession.

"Jersey City" and "wilderness" aren't commonly matched in word associations, but in this densely populated slice of Hudson County, an accident of history has allowed an almost invisible oasis to exist in the middle of the city for almost its entire history.

For Latham, a restaurateur on hiatus from the business, it has become his loving mission to preserve the space.

"Here was this beautiful wild spot, not manicured, not planted, but planted by nature," he explains. "It was this beautiful, very special place."

The wonder of God's creation is all around us. Respect it. Admire it.

How desirable are all His works, and how sparkling they are to see! (Sirach 42:22)

Holy Creator, inspire us to us to preserve and protect the works of Your hands.

When Enemies become Friends

John Rich and Takeo Sato first met when Sato was a prisoner of war and Rich, his interrogator.

The two had been combatants in a battle between American and Japanese forces on the island of Saipan during WWII. When Sato was captured, he feared the worst.

"I expected…someone would hit me," Sato said of his experience as a prisoner. "But John-san was a real gentleman."

Sato was soon moved to a prison camp in Hawaii, near where Rich was stationed. Rich began to visit him, and when Sato was released, Rich tracked him down in Japan. They continued to visit each other for over six decades, long after Rich had left the military and was no longer stationed in Japan. Now grandfathers, their families are forever bonded.

"Wars end," Rich said of their friendship. "People can get along right, if you treat them right."

If you forgive others their trespasses, your heavenly Father will also forgive you. (Matthew 6:14)

Lord, help me to see the good in all Your people.

Transforming Tragedy

One terrible day in 1998, Linda Ginzel got news no mother should ever have to hear: A portable crib had collapsed at the home of her licensed day-care provider, strangling her 17-month-old son Danny.

The day after Danny's funeral, Ginzel found while reading the *Chicago Tribune*, that Danny was the fifth child to die in a Playskool Travel-Lite crib, and the second since its recall in 1993.

Shocked that the government didn't require manufacturers to test children's products prior to sale, Linda and her husband founded Kids in Danger, an organization that advocates safety in children's products through a newsletter and lobbying.

With a push from Kids in Danger, seven states have passed laws banning the sale of recalled products. The long-term goal is to eliminate the need for children's product recalls.

The aftermath of tragedy can be to lose hope—or to work for hope-filled change.

Hoping against hope, (Abraham) believed that he would become 'the father of many nations'. (Romans 4:18)

When I am surrounded by despair, send me Your hopefulness, Savior.

Lesson in a Dog's Tale

In one Queens, New York, neighborhood, there's a good-looking visitor wandering the streets, a caramel colored German shepherd dog. This canine has no collar or home but plenty of concerned guardians.

"Everybody knows about him," says Angela Ferrini, one area resident. "He's calm and chilled out." She even named the dog, "Babe," when she tired hearing others refer to him as "the stray" or simply "the dog."

Mike Ibanescu, a cabdriver from Romania, often sees Babe in the morning. He puts food out for him, sometimes boiled beef.

Local animal authorities didn't have any record of a missing dog matching Babe's description. They hoped to find a home for him perhaps even in his current neighborhood.

In the meantime, the residents on the streets where Babe lives for now have taught us to look out for our neighbor and to reach out to the lost–human or animal.

O Lord, how manifold are your works! In wisdom You have made them all; the earth is full of Your creatures. (Psalm 104:24)

Creator, remind us to be kind to each other, to ourselves and to other creatures because we are all seeking acceptance and a home.

Dealing with the Fallout

Radioactive fallout from nuclear tests in Yucca Flat, Nevada between 1951 and 1962 drifted over 21 counties in Nevada, Arizona and Utah. Nineteen different cancers are the legacy of these tests among downwind-from-the-test-site residents.

Although the people of Emmett, Idaho, had been exposed to more iodine-131 than others, they were not offered the $50,000 compensation given to other "downwinders" by the U. S. Government. Sherri Garmon wrote to state legislator Kathy Skippen and she went to veteran reporter Janet Monti. A newspaper awareness campaign led to citizens speaking up and the National Academy of Sciences taking notice. Now it is up to Congress to decide whether or not to compensate the people of Emmett.

Every act has consequences. Governments and individuals should prayerfully weigh the consequences of every decision.

Wisdom is a fountain of life to one who has it, but folly is the punishment of fools. (Proverbs 16:22)

Holy Spirit, enable men, women — and governments — always to choose the ethical, the just, the good.

A Different Kind of Education

In September, 2004, the remnants of Hurricane Ivan hit Pittsburgh and its surrounding areas with unexpected fury. Massive flooding caused damage that took months to repair.

Among those who mobilized to help were the students of St. Malachy's School. The local Catholic elementary school spent a month collecting donations for the Greater Pittsburgh Community Food Bank. They focused their efforts on helping the students of St. Elizabeth Ann Seton, another local school so badly damaged by the floods that for months classes had to be held in another building.

The St. Malachy's food drive was ultimately even more successful than had been hoped. "They raised boxes and boxes and boxes and boxes" of food, St. Malachy's Chris Crytzer said of the students' efforts.

Even the youngest of us can make the world a better place. What can you do today?

Let the little children come to Me...for it is to such as these that the kingdom of God belongs. (Mark 10:14)

Blessed Trinity, help me to always see opportunities for helping others.

A Drive for Justice

Peter Malkin lost his sister, nephew and other relatives to the Nazi's monstrous "Final Solution" during World War II.

That fact, and a desire for justice, drove Malkin when he was recruited into the Mossad, the Israeli intelligence agency. Malkin rose through the ranks, and was eventually assigned to find former Nazis hiding in Argentina. While there, he led the team that tracked Adolf Eichmann, former head of Hitler's Department of Jewish Affairs and chief architect of the Holocaust. Malkin personally arrested the notorious war criminal himself.

Malkin's drive led to the trial and conviction of one of the worst mass-murderers in history, bringing a measure of justice to the 6-million Jews killed in Nazi death camps.

It's inevitable that each of us will experience tragedy in our lives. What's up to us is how we respond. We can let it stop us, or we can transform it into the impetus for constructive change.

To (Israelites) belong the adoption, the glory, the covenants, the giving of the law, the worship, and the promises...the patriarchs, and from them, according to the flesh, comes the Messiah. (Romans 9:4-5)

Lord, help me find meaning even in life's darkest moments.

Do Talk to Strangers

Victoria Bahr talks to "invisible people."

This does not involve séances in a candle-filled room or getting up early to search a dewy forest for leprechauns. What it does require is simply taking time to acknowledge the existence of people who stand patiently on the sidelines of our lives.

For Bahr that has meant conversations with the groundskeeper and maids at a hotel, the woman at the bus stop, and the cashier at the grocery store.

"Each one of us needs to receive acknowledgment and appreciation; it's as basic to life as food and water," explains Bahr. "It takes so little effort to notice people in our frame of reference. What a shame to treat them as if they are invisible! What a missed opportunity to make a difference in someone's life!"

But what a golden chance through those conversations to glimpse the God-given spark within every heart we meet.

In everything do to others as you would have them do to you; for this is the law and the prophets. (Matthew 7:12)

Thank You, Abba, for each person whose path crosses mine today.

Leading Service

When Mary Hallaren died in 2005, at age of 97, her death was announced by the Women's Hall of Fame in Seneca Falls, New York. A long, groundbreaking career in the U.S. Army earned her membership there in 1996.

Born in Lowell Massachusetts, Hallaren was a certified remedial reading instructor before she instinctively followed her brothers in enlisting. "To me," she said, "there was no question that women should serve."

Colonel Hallaren commanded the first battalion of the Women's Army Auxiliary Corps to serve in Europe in World War II. After the war, Hallaren helped to persuade Congress to pass the Women's Armed Services Integration Act bringing women into the regular armed services for the first time in U.S. history.

Male or female, we each have a uniquely constructive service to offer our nation. What is yours?

Speak the truth to one another, render... judgments that are true and make for peace, do not devise evil in your hearts against one another, and love no false oath; for all these are things that I hate, says the Lord. (Zechariah 8:16-17)

May I advance Your way of peace with toleration, respect and justice, Lord of All.

One Child, One Vote

A new educational movement is instilling a love of democracy in children like never before. "Democratic schools" aim to give children a say and a vote in how they are educated.

The Sudbury Valley School near Boston is one such school. Students there are given an opportunity to vote on their daily activities as well as their curriculum. Not surprisingly, the students vote in favor of play-like activities as a way to learn.

While critics might find this approach unworkable, supporters disagree. Jerry Mintz, director of the Alternative Education Resource Organization, says, "The bottom line is that these schools respect students' rights and the right to take control of their own education."

How do you handle disagreements with others? One way to tackle differences is to learn as much as possible about the opposing side's viewpoint. An informed opinion garners more respect than one that is not well-thought through.

Love does not wrong to a neighbor; therefore, love is the fulfilling of the law. (Romans 13:10)

May I respect others' opinions, and learn to disagree peacefully, Lord.

Always Leave Yourself Laughing

Studies abound on the connection between staying happy and staying healthy. Scientific proof shows that laughter strengthens the immune system and lowers levels of stress hormones as well as blood pressure.

Psychologist Steve Sultanoff says that laughter also appears to boost the body's production of infection-fighting antibodies. Laughter is also linked to increasing one's tolerance for pain.

So what are some things to add to your daily "to do" list to keep that laughter prescription filled? Rent a funny movie. Go to a comedy show. Listen to funny audiotapes or read a humorous book while commuting. Take the time to be silly.

And when all else fails, remember that God loves you. That is always a reason to smile.

When the Lord restored the fortunes of Zion... then our mouth was filled with laughter, and our tongue with shouts of joy. (Psalm 126:1,2)

With You, Father, I find joy and all good things.

A Life of Invention

Sixteen-year-old Andrew Toti loved working on his new boat, but his mother fretted that her son would be in danger out on the open water.

To assuage his mother's fears, Toti developed modifications to a life vest that could be strapped on and filled with air to keep the wearer afloat. During World War II, the War Department began equipping U.S. soldiers with a version of the same vest credited to Toti.

Those vests played a role in saving the lives of countless military men, including future president George H.W. Bush, who thanked Toti after he was shot down and forced to make use of the vest. Toti, meanwhile, went on to hold patents for over 500 other inventions, from grape harvesters to endotracheal tubes.

When Toti designed his version of a life vest, he may have thought he was only comforting his mother, but he also paved the way for a lifetime of innovation. Taking worthwhile action is the best response to any situation.

**The clever do all things intelligently.
(Proverbs 13:16)**

Spirit of Courage, provide me with the bravery to innovate.

Waiting for the School Mule

Every morning, Saje Beard commutes to her one-room schoolhouse with Ruth—or rather, *on* Ruth, a gray mule.

The Bismarck, North Dakota, third-grader has been making the half-hour "mule run" since first grade. "I feel safer with her riding a mule than having her ride in a car or on a bus," says her father, Marty. In the colder weather, though, these other transportation methods are utilized.

At the Manning School, Saje "parks" Ruth by tying her to a tree near swing sets and monkey bars. Her classmates help take off Ruth's saddle and tack, storing them in the school's cloakroom, next to basketballs and other playground equipment.

The trip home on Ruth seems to move faster, says Saje, who's convinced her mule knows there's grain awaiting her at home.

Whether by mule or another way, there are many ways to reach a goal in life. What's important is to attain it.

I will...teach you the way you should go. ...Do not be like a horse or a mule, without understanding, whose temper must be curbed with bit and bridle, else it will not stay near you. (Psalm 32:8,9)

Abba, protect children wherever they go.

Choosing Life

Anger at the perpetrator is an understandable reaction for parents whose child has been murdered.

When Sherri and Seth Mandell's 13-year-old son Koby and a friend were stoned to death by Arabs in Israel, their adopted country, they grieved. But they also tried to be faithful to Deuteronomy 30:19 where God says: "I have set before you life and death, blessings and curse; therefore choose life, that you and your descendants may live."

The Mandells directed their anguish in a positive direction by starting a foundation in remembrance of their son. It runs Camp Koby for youngsters who have lost their parents or siblings to terror. Participants have many opportunities to enjoy therapeutic art, music and drama. Various religious, ethnic and cultural groups get involved.

It's not easy. "Each day, I have to work to go on," notes Sherri Mandell.

Whatever happens, keep hope in your heart.

Did not your father eat and drink and do justice and righteousness? Then it was well with him. ...Is not this to know Me? says the Lord. (Jeremiah 22:15,16)

Holy Spirit, give me hope.

For Life and Forgiveness

Victoria Thorn was still in college when a friend had an abortion. "I tried to help," she said, "but never knew how to reach her and I could not seem to say the right things."

Years later, she became a counselor for a crisis pregnancy center and eventually became one of the first experts on post abortion ministry. She started Project Rachel and became executive director of the National Office of Post-Abortion Reconciliation and Healing.

She and others who volunteer in church-related groups around the country try to help mothers and fathers who are coming to terms with the trauma that abortion can cause.

Victoria Thorn is firmly convinced that healing is possible, even for those who have kept the pain hidden for years. Forgiveness of self and others is a vital part of the process.

Forgiveness is one of the most important gifts you can give or receive. Open your heart.

Forgive and you will be forgiven. (Luke 6:37)

Divine Lord, forgive us our sins and help us to forgive others and ourselves as well.

Overcoming Tragedy Through Faith

Helen Siegel, an award-winning artist, printmaker and illustrator, grew up under the horrific conditions of war-torn Vienna in the 1930's and 1940's. She remembers her family hiding hunted Jews from the Gestapo, listening to the screams of classmates trapped in a wine cellar after a bombing, and fighting with a cousin over a meager scrap of food.

Siegel found a way to overcome the horrors she faced. "Suffering...strengthened our faith... bringing us closer to God," she said. Worshipping at St. Stephen's Cathedral "provided a visual escape and a hope for eternal things." Her dedication to her art and to God helped her through those difficult times.

Tragedy and hard times are part of every human life, but our faith helps us triumph over adversity. Turn to God, and let times of suffering bring you closer to Him. Your faith can turn such trials into a beautiful testimony.

Come to Me, all you that are weary and are carrying heavy burdens, and I will give you rest. (Matthew 11:28)

Gentle Jesus, please help me to turn to You in times of hardship.

The Lessons of History

Is accurate history possible?

Nat Turner, subject of numerous books and articles since his 1831 hanging, is seen as both heroic leader and fanatic villain depending on who is telling his story.

Turner, enslaved in Virginia, led a 19th century revolt against slavery. According to a *New York Times* story it was the bloodiest slave rebellion in American history.

"Nat Turner is a classic example of an iconic figure who is deeply heroic on one side and deeply villainous on the other," said Yale history professor David W. Blight.

As the *Times* says, "For those who need a slave rebel, he serves that purpose. For those who need to see him as a deranged revolutionary who likes slaughtering people, they can see that, too.

"He's forever our own invention in some ways" given the paucity of evidence about him.

Ask questions. Study history critically. Consider your own biases as well as that of historians. Above all, think for yourself.

Do not judge by appearances. (John 7:24)

Refresh our minds' critical faculties, Holy Spirit, so that we may be intelligent readers and thinkers.

Canine Champion

Leana Beasley initially felt fine the morning she suffered an epileptic seizure, but Faith, her specially-trained Rottweiler, could evidently sense that something was amiss. She shadowed her owner all day, refusing to let Beasley out of her sight.

Faith's obstinacy proved to be well-founded, as later in the day, Beasley fell to the ground, incapacitated. Luckily, Faith was trained for just such an occurrence.

The dog quickly nudged the telephone off the hook and used her nose to hit the speed-dial button programmed for 911. She barked into the receiver to signal that her owner needed help, and then even managed to unlock the front door for the responding emergency personnel.

Even the most unexpected creature can contribute to the good of the world. Never underestimate the people–or pets–around you.

Rejoice in doing good. (Jeremiah 32:41)

Lord, let me see the potential in everyone.

Inspirational Heroes

What makes someone heroic in the eyes of others?

- Lance Armstrong, a seven-time winner of the Tour de France bicycle race, faced his own mortality when he was diagnosed with metastasized stage-four testicular cancer at age 26.

"I spent many years before I got sick wondering what I was going to do, and it was a distraction. I know what I am doing this year and next, and they deserve my attention." In addition to the Tour de France, Armstrong is focused on his family and his cancer research foundation.

- A devout Muslim judge in her fifties, Shirin Ebadi has long struggled for equality for women, children, workers and artists in Iran. Many find the 2003-Nobel-Peace-Prize winner inspirational.

"When you are hopeless," she says, "you are at a dead end."

Be a hero. Serve God by serving others.

Hope does not disappoint us. (Romans 5:5)

Whether it's disease, the rights of those in need, or any other difficult situation, Holy Spirit, keep us courageously hope-filled in our search for a solution.

Fighting Oppression

People often have a way of using ingenuity to overcome their oppression by others.

For centuries, women in China were denied an education and its benefits. That isolated women, so some learned to communicate secretly in a script known as Nushu or "female writing". Nushu is a language used exclusively by women "to share feminine feelings including fears about arranged marriages, husbands, and, of course, mothers-in-law."

Yang Huanyi was the last woman to use it under the traditional oath of secrecy. She was in her late 90s when she died in 2004 in China's Hunan Province.

According to one academic, "What started as a simple way to express themselves became a chronicle of their private anguish."

It also was a way to cope with pain. "By writing, so much suffering disappears," Yang once said in an interview.

Ease the troubles of others through your kindness and friendship.

Bear one another's burdens. (Galatians 6:2)

Joys shared are doubled; sorrows, halved. Encourage us, therefore, to share our feelings with trusted friends, Divine Creator.

Off the Air to Take the Field

If you tuned in to Nickelodeon television network one Saturday in October from noon to 3 p.m. EST, you'd have found—well, nothing.

Instead of the traditional children's programming, the network instead called for a "worldwide day of play."

"Nickelodeon wants YOU to GET UP, GET OUT and PLAY!" proclaimed the message on the television screen during that three-hour period.

This tuning out to tune in to life outside the box—the television, that is—seemed just what kids wanted. The hours after the "no television" time were filled with across-the-country reports on the healthy, outdoor activities young people had enjoyed with friends and family.

So next time you reach for the remote control on a beautiful Saturday afternoon, put it down—and grab the door knob instead.

You stretch out the heavens like a tent...You set the earth on its foundations...You have made the moon to mark the seasons; the sun knows its time for setting....the earth is full of your creatures. (Psalm 104:2,5,19)

Creator, remind us to make time to enjoy the beauty of Your world through out-of-doors activities.

Honesty Champs: Kids Turn in Tickets

New York Yankees. Playoff tickets. Box seats. Free. Could you resist?

Well, the tickets weren't exactly free–some cost as much as $2,600. They belonged to a bank and apparently fell off a delivery truck in New Jersey. Several youngsters found them and turned them over to the police.

"We do have a lot of good kids out there, and that's why their actions should be commended," said Detective Lt. Robert Wreck.

"It's a real tribute to their honesty and total integrity," said Yankees owner George Steinbrenner.

The youngsters were rewarded with tickets to games for themselves and their parents as well as Yankee memorabilia. And they were honored at City Hall.

Of course, their parents are hoping their children have learned that honesty is it's own reward.

Birds roost with their own kind, so honesty comes home to those who practice it. (Sirach 27:9)

Abba, help parents be living examples of honesty.

How We Can "Support Our Troops"

Chris Carney visited Walter Reed Army Medical Center and found that members of the military recovering from injuries received in Iraq lacked support and necessities. Moreover, "these kids...are scared of what's next, of how they're going to feed their families," Carney said.

Deciding to make the ubiquitous "Support Our Troops" slogan meaningful, Carney arranged a coast-to-coast bicycle trek and raised hundreds of thousands of dollars for the Wounded Warriors Project.

"Chris made it possible for us to pay for 2,400 backpacks (each containing a CD player, clothes and toiletries)–two years' worth–plus pay the salary of a full-time counselor at Walter Reed to help the disabled vets with benefits and jobs," said Wounded Warriors founder John Melia.

In the words of President Lincoln, what can you do "to care for him (and her) who shall have borne the battle?"

Come you that are blessed by My Father...for I was sick and you took care of Me. (Matthew 25:34,36)

God, we lose the treasure of our young men and women in war. Show us how to find peace and justice.

Discovering New Talents

For most Americans, Julia Child is a household name synonymous with French cuisine, fine dining and a gloriously unconventional way of cooking. What many people don't know is that Julia Child was 32 years old before she learned how to cook.

When she met her husband Paul in 1944, food didn't matter much to her. However, to please her husband, she learned to cook, earning a diploma at France's Cordon Bleu while Paul was stationed in Paris during World War II.

With the help of two French colleagues, Julia Child wrote *Mastering the Art of French Cooking* in 1961, and had her own TV show within two years, charming her American audience with her realistic, humorous approach to the craft of cooking.

It's never to late to learn a new skill. Human beings are blessed with incredible ability. It's up to you as an individual to find your talents and develop them.

A capable wife...is far more precious than jewels. (Proverbs 31:10)

Lord, help me to discover and to use the talents with which You have blessed me.

Advice for Newlyweds

In an article in *Marriage* magazine, Carolyn Vinup offers some words of advice for newlyweds. Here are a few of her tips:

- Laugh, hug and touch every day.
- Look your loved one in the eyes and say "I love you." Keep looking…
- Give up the Power/Control game right away. Apologize after a fight; forgive and then let it go. And always, listen more than you talk.
- Make your marriage a priority and schedule regular dates. Simplify your life; remember who and what are important.
- Surrender with your heart; love grows deeper when you do.

These tips will work well for long-married couples, too. What can you add to this list from your own experiences?

Let marriage be held in honor by all. (Hebrews 13:4)

Keep us honest, loyal and loving in all our relationships, Faithful Savior.

Think You Know Helen Keller?

It bothers teacher and writer Ruth Shagoury Hubbard that Helen Keller is depicted in most children's books simply as "a brilliant deaf and blind woman who surmounted incredible obstacles."

Keller, born into a wealthy Alabama family in 1880, triumphed over major disabilities partly because of "the advantages of my birth and environment."

But Hubbard says, "Here is a woman who worked tirelessly as a radical advocate for the poor, but she is depicted as a kind of saintly role model for people with handicaps."

Hubbard thinks more could be done to convey her courage: she studied speech to more effectively "promote the social justice she believed in." She supported women's right to vote as well as unions. She questioned why a wealthy nation tolerated great poverty. And after visiting Hiroshima and Nagasaki, she recommitted herself to the anti-war movement.

There's more to most people than meets the eye. Look for it.

Many women have done excellently, but you surpass them all. (Proverbs 31:29)

Thank You, Redeemer, for courageous people who work for the common good.

Changing the Face of Hansen's Disease

Dr. Paul Brand, a pioneer in orthopedic reconstructive surgery, never lived in Beverly Hills, had celebrity patients or earned millions of dollars.

Instead, Dr. Paul Brand went to India in the 1940s to help people with Hansen's Disease (leprosy) whose hands had become deformed. Later he adapted his surgery to help patients with diabetes, which, like leprosy, deadens pain sensations.

At the same time, his wife, Dr. Margaret Brand, conducted research on preventing blindness in people with Hansen's Disease.

The Doctors Brand spent nearly 20 years in India, helping alleviate suffering. Their legacy lives on in Dr. Paul Brand's book, *Clinical Mechanics of the Hand,* a reference work for hand surgeons, physical therapists and other hand specialists.

The path to genuine success and fulfillment has little to do with fortune and fame. How can you use your gifts to help others?

The price of wisdom is above pearls. ...nor can it be valued in pure gold. (Job 28:18,19)

Heavenly Father, give me the wisdom to realize that money cannot buy either happiness or fulfillment.

Instant Pleasure?

Satellite TV, cable, cell phones, TiVo, iPods, remote control. Technology is great, right? Not so fast.

Writing in *The New Atlantis,* editor and historian Christine Rosen cautions about being seduced into a pleasure addiction. Some get hooked beginning with the TV remote which is "light, easily manipulated with one hand, and responds to any immediate whim with the merest physical effort."

She makes the point that technological devices have altered our egos, attention spans, critical thinking, social discourse, and appreciation of art.

Attention spans are shorter. Boredom is up. Intellectual curiosity is down. Rosen says, "when things become instantly accessible, they lose value."

Since technology is here to stay, set limits. Put down the remote and the headphones. Limit TV viewing. When in public spaces, don't stay wired for private conversation or entertainment.

Think for yourself. Use the mind God gave you for your good and that of those around you.

Get wisdom; get insight. (Proverbs 4:5)

Holy Trinity, remind us of the importance of social and intellectual interactions.

When to Say "No"

There are times when the most positive thing you can do is say "No."

Dr. Frances Kelsey knew that. In 1960, she was a new drug evaluator for the U.S. Food and Drug Administration. Her first assignment was to assess a drug which could help induce sleep and also relieve morning sickness for pregnant women. Because it was already widely used in Europe, Dr. Kelsey was being pressured by the drug company for quick approval.

But the doctor found serious flaws in the data concerning the drug's toxicity and manufacturing quality control. Dr. Kelsey withheld approval. By the end of the year, reports began to surface from other countries of babies born with serious deformities to mothers who had used the drug.

Thanks to one woman with courage, thalidomide never caused the devastation in America that it had elsewhere.

Even when it's difficult, say "No" to what you honestly believe to be wrong.

Judge with right judgment. (John 7:24)

Protect us, Merciful Lord, from harm to body or soul. And may we never willingly hurt ourselves or any other child of Yours.

Extending Your Reach

"I was a teenager when I learned how to rope calves...Rope is a tool, very macho, not like a whip, but something magical that allows you to control things way beyond your reach," says James Garvey, a blacksmith artist who forges sculptures for public spaces.

Garvey's "Lariat Seat Loops" and "Lariat Handrail" adorn New York City subway stations.

"Though Mr. Garvey's artifacts are heavy, some look light because of their sinuous shapes, especially the pieces that appear to be made of rope," according to a story in the *New York Times*.

The ropelike forms "were inspired by images that made an impression on Garvey in his youth..." much of which he had spent in Colorado.

Knowing how to control things beyond your reach can be useful. Knowing how to extend that knowledge to other areas of your life is even more useful.

The wise lay up knowledge. (Proverbs 10:14)

Holy Spirit, show me how to use the knowledge I have in one field in others.

Going by the Rule

When you consider how frustrating, difficult, even painful life can be, the number of people who go out of their way for others is amazing. Not everybody or every time, of course; still, many go the extra mile. Some people have a keen sensitivity to the needs and feelings of others.

Judith Martin, also known as Miss Manners, said, "Putting yourself in another person's place means imagining that person's point of view, not just thinking of what you with your ideas would do in the other person's situation."

She's really talking about the Golden Rule at its best: "Do unto others as you would have them do unto you." What we want done to us is to have someone give us the help we need when we need it—and with the empathy and generosity that make all the difference.

And that's the most important rule you can ever follow.

You shall love the Lord your God with all your heart, and with all your soul, and with all your strength, and with all your mind; and your neighbor as yourself. (Luke 10:27)

Let the Golden Rule be the measure of my life, Gracious Father.

Raising Tolerant Children

In a world of diversity, we need tolerance. "Sensitivity to difference starts as early as infancy," notes Dr. T. Berry Brazelton, professor emeritus of pediatrics at Harvard Medical School. Lessons in tolerance must also begin early.

The noted pediatrician advises parents to prepare for those inevitable times when their children remark on differences. This typically peaks in the fifth year and again in early adolescence.

A five year old might ask: "Why is your hair yellow? Can I touch it?" Brazelton says "our responses can be critical in setting the stage for tolerance. 'Each of us is unique. You have straight blond hair. Alice has curly black hair.' 'You are left-handed; Ethan is right-handed'."

"Self-acceptance is the cornerstone for all tolerance and appreciation of differences in others," writes Dr. Brazelton.

Differences and biases need to be acknowledged. Value your own ethnic, cultural and social groups without denigrating others'.

You have heard that it was said, "You shall love your neighbor and hate your enemy." But I say to you, Love your enemies and pray for those who persecute you." (Matthew 5:43-44)

Creator, help us delight in differences even as You obviously do.

Tackling Daily Chores, Quickly

The quicker you take care of tedious household chores the more time you'll have for your family, friends and life's pleasantries.

"When we try to do too much at once we can feel paralyzed and overwhelmed," says time-management expert Ellen Kosloff. Instead, break big jobs into smaller tasks. Or keep jobs from becoming too big in the first place. Here are other suggestions from *Family Circle* magazine to help you whittle down your "to-do list:"

- open the mail next to a recycling container; toss the junk
- fold each item right out of the dryer
- put grocery store purchases away as soon as you get home
- double dinner recipes and freeze half for another night
- pack school bags and briefcases and lay out clothes the night before

As you gain free time, consider how to use it wisely and well.

For everything there is a season and a time for every matter under heaven. (Ecclesiastes 3:1)

Remind us, Jesus, to enjoy, to savor, each moment of the time that is Your gift to us.

Sharing the Most Precious Gift

"Mom, if you're alive when I go, I want you to donate my organs," 13-year-old Heidi Sewalish said to her mother Dianne while watching a TV program on the subject.

Just weeks later Heidi was killed in a car accident. Dianne Sewalish said she would donate her daughter's organs. Though it was excruciating to lose her child, donating her organs allowed something positive to come out of terrible tragedy. "It gives her death meaning as opposed to it just being senseless," said Dianne Sewalish.

Heidi's kidneys, liver, left lung, corneas and heart went to ailing recipients. Sewalish later met some of them, including the 60-year-old man who received Heidi's heart.

"Can I hear my daughter's heart?" Dianne asked. "Of course," said the recipient who said he felt humbled "and grateful that she was generous enough to donate."

The gift of renewed life through donated organs or blood is admirable. Value life everyday.

**What must I do to inherit eternal life?
(Luke 10:25)**

Merciful Savior, show us how to help others.

Experiencing Poverty

Can people who are financially very comfortable appreciate what it's like to live in a shack and in poverty?

Members of Habitat For Humanity International, a non-denominational Christian ministry that builds low-cost housing worldwide, are trying to increase people's understanding.

They opened the Global Village and Discovery Center, an unlikely tourist attraction, in Americus, Georgia in 2003. The 30 shacks duplicate the poor housing in Africa, Asia and Central America, though not the smells, stagnant water or dangers which might keep visitors, and donations, away.

"It's a before-and-after of poverty housing," said Millard Fuller, Habitat's president and founder.

After touring the run down shacks, visitors are led through model houses similar to those Habitat volunteers build.

Remaining sensitive to others' poverty and inadequate housing means re-evaluating one's own housing and living more simply.

God gives the desolate a home. (Psalm 68:6)

Abba, remind us that there can not be true peace as long as most of the world's people live in hovels and lack even life's necessities.

A Unique Retirement Home

"I just decided that the old guy had worked all his life and deserved a little rest and comfort during his final years," said Michelle Feldstein. "I had no intention of starting a blasted retirement home."

She isn't talking about a retirement home for older men and women, but for horses and other large animals past their prime. Once their usefulness as work animals has ended, Feldstein and her husband Al shelter them at their Montana ranch for elderly animals.

Her actions on behalf of these elderly, infirm or abused animals and her tender loving care, belie Feldstein's somewhat brusque remarks. She names each animal whom she feeds, cleans and pets daily.

A tender regard for all creatures goes hand-in-hand with a tender regard for one's fellow human beings and is a sign of sound mental and emotional health.

God said, "Let the waters bring forth swarms of living creatures, and let birds fly...And God said, "Let the earth bring forth living creatures...cattle and creeping things and wild animals." (Genesis 1:20,24)

Creator, thank You sincerely for life's amazing, astounding diversity. Help us be awed and hushed to reverence by it.

Rise and Shine and Make a Difference

Janet Trinkaus took her personal experience and her professional skills as a marketing executive and created Rise n' Shine, an organization that helps youngsters whose parents have AIDS.

"I had no volunteer experience, but I had been around kids all my life. I knew I had an intuitive sense about what kids needed. I wrote a design for a camp that mimicked my own childhood summer camp," said Trinkaus.

"There would be a mentor program that could guide these kids the way my favorite aunt had guided me; holiday get-togethers like the ones at my grandma's where 40 or 50 of us would gather; support groups like those I'd found at my church.

"It was the supportive environment I knew these kids would have a hard time finding."

Through the lean and difficult times, Trinkaus kept going. She overcame prejudice and fear and changed lives.

Never be afraid to do good.

Happy are those who persevere. (Daniel 12:12)

Jesus, guide me in helping people, not judging them.

Shed No Tears for the Onion

Did you ever think the onion was "sacred"? Ancient Egyptians did. Onions were represented in many tomb paintings and even buried with royalty. The bulb symbolized the universe to the Egyptians, who thought the spheres of heaven, earth and hell were concentric, like onion layers.

The Egyptians also regarded onions as a cure-all and a dietary necessity for workers building the pyramids. The Greek historian Herodotus wrote that pharaohs once spent nine tons of gold for onions to feed laborers. Honey-and-onion sandwiches were once a workingman's lunch.

In the centuries since, this sacred food has been highly regarded by folk healers as a natural antibiotic. Onions help treat edema, worms, warts, and boils; they may even prevent hair loss and protect against cancer.

The next time you enjoy onion on a burger or in a salad, take a minute to think of its illustrious history—and remember that not everything is as it seems.

We remember the fish we used to eat in Egypt for nothing, the cucumbers, the melons, the leeks, the onions, and the garlic. (Numbers 11:5)

Help me savor the good things in life, Lord, and enjoy the beauty of Your creation.

Kitchen Table Wisdom

Woman's Day editors asked readers for some good advice they'd heard at their kitchen tables. Here are some:

- "It's better to be kind than to be right."
- "Always have a box of stationery handy for sending impromptu thank-you cards."
- "People believe what you believe about yourself. If you walk out of a room thinking you're hot stuff, they'll believe it, too!"
- "Never say, 'I told you so' to your husband, even when you told him so."
- "You can choose to be a dieter or you can choose to be an athlete. Choosing to be an athlete means you commit to health, fitness and nutritious eating. Food becomes fuel. You don't beat yourself up for eating occasional treats."

Search for wisdom—wonderful wisdom.

If you desire wisdom, keep the commandments and the Lord will lavish her upon you. (Sirach 1:26)

Holy Spirit, enlighten us, guide us, abide with us.

Earning Trust

"It looked like a play space," said one mother seeking help for her abused child at a Safe Horizon program in Brooklyn on the advice her pediatrician.

And Detective Anthony DeMaria was just what the doctor ordered. DeMaria, married with four children, works in the delicate and difficult field of child abuse investigation. He is successful, too, if awards from colleagues and the trust of children are any indication.

It's DeMaria's job to investigate allegations of abuse, find the truth, and bring perpetrators to justice. For this, he has to be able to develop a rapport with possible abusers and with kids.

The detective might wear a Muppet puppet on his hand, chat about Sponge Bob or color for half an hour if it helps a child to relax enough to tell him their often-horrific stories of abuse.

"If you can help one kid, you've done enough," says DeMaria. What can you do to prevent the abuse of children?

If any of you put a stumbling block before one of these little ones who believe in Me, it would be better for you if a great millstone were fastened around your neck and you were drowned in...the sea. (Matthew 18:6)

Just Judge, help us end child abuse.

Changing the World With a Cuisinart

The usual rhythm of women pounding grains and nuts into breakfast, lunch and dinner with heavy wooden pestles has been replaced in one village in Mali. These African women instead press a button, letting a mechanical grinder/blender—a giant "Cuisinart," of sorts—do the job. The machine reduces a day-long job to a mere 10-minute one.

"It's changing our lives," said Mineta Keita, president of a women's association which manages the machine and the flourishing businesses that have sprouted around it.

Mothers and daughters who would have spent a lifetime just preparing food for the family now have free time to take literacy courses, start up family businesses, expand family farming plots, and nurture a cash crop such as rice.

Sometimes overcoming everyday challenges can have life-changing results. What in your life needs changing? Start now!

Unless you change and become like children, you will never enter the kingdom of heaven. Whoever becomes humble like this child is greatest in the kingdom of heaven. (Matthew 18:3-4)

We place our trust in You, Loving Lord. From You come all good things.

It's a Bird! It's a Plane! It's a Doctor!

In one part of Idaho, waiting to see the doctor means watching the skies. Dr. Richard Paris, a family physician, flies his own Cessna 210 over the Idaho mountains to bring comprehensive medical care to more than 4,000 Custer County residents.

In 2005, Dr. Paris was named "doctor of the year" by the 2005 American Academy of Family Physicians (AAFP). Seeing him as a standout in an age of super-specialized HMO health care providers, Dr. Paris was cited particularly for "giving of himself beyond the medicine," explained Dr. Mary Frank, AAFP president. "He does everything a family doctor should do but often under adverse circumstances."

Explains Dr. Paris: "It's not about a single surgery or a broken leg. It's a lifelong relationship with patients."

In life, getting the job done sometimes requires going the extra mile or exploring new roads—even skyways.

There may come a time when recovery lies in the hands of physicians, for they too pray to the Lord that He grant them success in diagnosis and in healing, for the sake of preserving life. (Sirach 38;13-14)

Bless physicians and all health care workers, Lord of Life.

Appreciating the Past

As she approached age 100, Emma Buck was still sharpening axes, drawing well water and walking to the outhouse. She died in 2004 on her family's pre-Civil War farm.

"The Buck farmstead is a rare glimpse into the past," Mike Jackson, chief architect with the Illinois Historic Preservation Agency told the *New York Times*. "It is an extremely well-preserved place, maintained by a woman who lived a 19th-century life throughout the 20th century. Its significance is far greater than its humble origins."

And "to spend time with Miss Buck was to feel the evocative power of a place that has all but vanished...a fragile holdout where it was possible to encounter wooden butter churns, hobnail boots, copper kettles...and hoops for a Conestoga wagon", he added. There are plans to preserve the 70-acre-farm as a living history museum.

Ask family elders to talk about their lives. Knowledge of the past is a sound foundation for the present and future.

To the sensible person education is like a golden ornament. (Sirach 21:21)

God, may our lives reflect our gratitude for the diligence and hard work of our ancestors.

Do You Have a Daily Dozen?

Too few of us take the time to think through the values and moral precepts that guide our lives. Here is an edited version of writer Robert Louis Stevenson's (1850-1894) personal creed:

1. Make up your mind to be happy.
2. Make the best of your circumstances.
3. Don't take yourself too seriously.
4. Don't let criticism worry you.
5. Be yourself.
6. Stay out of debt.
7. Don't borrow trouble; imaginary troubles are hard to bear.
8. Don't hold grudges; avoid people who make you unhappy.
9. Have a variety of interests; go places or read about them.
10. Don't brood; get over it.
11. Help those less fortunate.
12. Keep busy; a busy person never has time to be unhappy.

What precepts are guiding you?

If you wish to enter into life, keep the commandments. (Matthew 19:17)

Teach me Your way of life, Holy Spirit.

What One Person Can Do—for So Many

Nearly 28,000 people have been touched by the efforts of one teenager.

Makenzie Snyder has been sending duffel bags and stuffed animals to foster children since she was seven. Her goal is to cheer up neglected children who are often shuffled between temporary homes.

Conducted through social workers, Makenzie Snyder's work has raised both funds and an awareness of the plight of foster children. Her efforts have raised about $50,000 in contributions.

When will her mission be complete? "I actually want to do it forever, until I help all the 530,000 foster care children in the United States," she says.

Children have much to offer the world. Support efforts and organizations that aim to protect children, particularly those that work to end child abuse or child labor law violations. Defending the defenseless is the noblest of causes.

"Let the little children come to Me; do not stop them." And He took them up in His arms, laid His hands on them, and blessed them. (Mark 10:14,16)

Jesus, who welcomed little children, protect the world's children from harm and suffering.

Saints among Us

Saints are holy people. Yet, the individual expression of that holiness varies greatly. What saints are not is average, even if the circumstance of their lives appear to be so.

Caryll Houselander, a spiritual writer and artist, put it this way: "The saints are a rebuke and a challenge hardly to be suffered, for their way is always the impractical way of the Sermon on the Mount: poverty, humility, the following of the Cross.

"And yet, when the years move on and we look back, we find that it is not the social reformer or the economist or even the church leader who has done tremendous things for the human race, but the silly saints in their rags and tatters, with their empty pockets and impossible dreams."

Express your faith, hope and love of God by giving yourself to the service of your brothers and sisters.

If you wish to enter into life, keep the Commandments. (Matthew 19:17)

Beloved Lord, thank You for Your holy servants. Help us follow their example as we live in Your loving presence.

Finding Faith in Death

When Chris' mom died, four years after his father's death, he felt as though his life was falling apart around him.

Then one afternoon while Chris was painting a neighborhood restaurant, his friend Ann stopped by. She, too, had lost both parents. An editor of a Catholic magazine, Ann offered Chris columns she had written about being an "adult orphan"; columns which spoke of the strength she drew from her own faith.

Two days later, Ann found a note in her mailbox from Chris. "It's comforting to know that others have the same feelings," he wrote. Speaking of coping with death through faith he mentioned missing it in his life. And, he added, "perhaps it's time to reconnect with faith. Thanks for reminding me."

Connecting with others, in joy and in sorrow, can make all the difference in their lives.

I will give you my support. (2 Samuel 3:12)

Send Your angels to those who mourn, Beloved God, that they may wrap them in wings filled with Your love.

Want to Change the World?

Susan Moon, editor of *Turning Wheel*, the journal of the Buddhist Peace Fellowship, says citizens have a responsibility to "get off their cushions and get involved." Here are her suggestions:

- Vote!
- Do the nitty-gritty, including helping to register voters.
- Support worthy causes, as you can.
- Read to educate yourself, and write letters to the editor, op-ed articles to inform others.
- Listen and talk to people, even those who don't agree with you.
- Share good news when it happens—and it does!
- Thank your elected representatives for courageous actions.
- Bear witness—always in a peaceful way.

It's your country. What have you done for it today?

Wisdom...is first pure, then peaceable, gentle, willing to yield, full of mercy and good fruits, without...partiality or hypocrisy...righteousness is sown in peace for those who make peace. (James 3:17,18)

God of justice, send Your peace to our nation; to our world.

Mickey Mouse Goes to College

The name Norman Baker may not ring any bells. Yet, he was the man behind the music heard by generations of children.

Baker, the composer of film and television scores including *The Mickey Mouse Club,* died in 2002 at the age of 84. At one point, almost 90 percent of the music played at Disney theme parks, including music for rides like It's a Small World and The Haunted Mansion, was composed by Baker.

He willed his musical magic to New York University, where he sometimes taught. NYU hopes the gift will draw attention not only to Baker's career, but also to other little known longtime Disney composers whose music entertained so many children.

Ronald Sadoff, NYU's director of film scoring, said that these composers "seemed to be able to connect America with something very moral and very primitive in our childhood."

Music is their legacy. What will yours be?

Wisdom is as good as an inheritance. (Ecclesiastes 7:11)

I praise You, Lord. You have done great things for me.

Finding Jesus' Boat

After 14 years of restoration, a simple wooden boat went on display at a center in Israel a few years ago.

Two brothers had discovered the remains of the ancient vessel in 1986 when a severe drought lowered the waters of the Sea of Galilee. The location of the brothers' find was just a few hundred yards from Migdal, the hometown of Mary called the Magdalene.

Tests dated the vessel to the first centuries after Jesus' birth. During the years of restoration and study, experts concluded that it was probably used by a crew of five people. They also suggested that this was most likely the type of boat used by Jesus' followers.

Although most of us will not unearth an ancient treasure, we all possess great riches, no matter how little we have. There are our relationships with those we love and who love us—and with God.

Make purses for yourselves that do not wear out, an unfailing treasure in heaven...For where your treasure is, there your heart will be also. (Luke 12:33,34)

Thanks, Master, for the gifts You send my way this day.

Once Lost and Now Found

When Michael Holman flew out to a deserted area of Alaska's Koyuktolik Bay, he expected a routine day's beachcombing, not an extreme test of his survival skills.

After landing, Holman's plane was destroyed by an incoming tide. There he was, stranded, at the edge of the Kenai Peninsula.

He had to manage alone for six days because adverse weather prevented his rescue. Because he was well equipped, Holman never let fear get the best of him. "I've got to be honest and say I never reached desperation stage," he said. Yet "that doesn't negate the absolute joy I felt at seeing the (rescue) helicopter this morning."

Sometimes in life we lose our way. Sometimes we have the survival skills to get back on track. Other times we need to be rescued. Hone your survival skills. And don't be too proud to accept help.

Your word is a lamp to my feet and a light to my path. (Psalm 119:105)

Guide me, Lord.

Too Busy or Tired To Vote? Never

"As we entered (New York) harbor my mother reminded me that I was an American citizen. I saw Lady Liberty standing there and I said to her, 'I will be a good citizen.' And I have been."

Gertrude Kern was born in the United States in 1907, but spent her childhood in England during the terrors of World War I. When she returned to the U.S. as a teenager, she started on the path that would lead to her vying at age 96 for a place in the *Guinness Book of World Records* as the world's oldest activist.

Always a voter, Kern spent decades campaigning and lobbying. She wrote letters to editors and spoke out particularly for world peace. Even a broken pelvis didn't stop her. She encouraged fellow rehabilitation patients with her optimistic view that activism beats apathy.

Citizenship is a responsibility. Exercise it today.

I am responsible for the lives of all.
(1 Samuel 22:22)

Redeemer, remind us that we citizens are responsible for each other's lives and freedoms.

R-E-S-P-E-C-T

"People who exercise power should do so carefully, fairly and sensitively," says a woman who is a high-powered New York attorney.

Unfortunately, while many people are careful, fair and sensitive, it's all to easy to find examples of the opposite behavior.

For instance, one supervisor walked into an employee's cubicle and wordlessly dived under his desk to access a power cord. Then the supervisor called the maintenance man who, in error, unplugged the employee's computer.

Only "auto save" protected an open document of hundreds of pages from total loss. The two co-workers just said, "accidents happen." And the employee was left feeling that neither he nor his work had been shown simple respect.

Employers, supervisors–all workers–have a responsibility to value and esteem each person with whom they work. In word and deed, treat those around you with the same respect you want for yourself.

Whoever wishes to become great among you must be your servant. (Mark 10:43)

Jesus, Son of Joseph the carpenter of Nazareth, help me see You in all with whom I work, and treat them accordingly.

The Happiest Choice You'll Ever Make

How many people do you know who go through life always seeing a glass that's half empty? What are their lives like?

They're probably negative, critical, pessimistic folks whom you go out of your way to avoid. On the other hand, there are the half full sort of people who exude optimism and positive thinking. These are the men and women we enjoy being around—and who enjoy their own company, as well.

While most of us say we want to be happy, too many of us spend more time pursuing the things we think will make us happy rather than simply choosing to be happy wherever and whatever we are. Just what is the relationship between attitude and happiness?

A wise man named Abraham Lincoln put it this way: "Most people are about as happy as they make up their minds to be."

Have you made up your mind yet?

This is what I have seen to be good: ...to eat and drink and find enjoyment in all the toil with which one toils. (Ecclesiastes 5:18)

Spirit of God, speak to me of Your presence in my life. Inspire me with Your joy and peace.

Unexpected Generosity

Marine Sgt. Joshua Horton was going through one of the darkest periods of his life in the fall of 2004. He'd been wounded by a mortar blast in Iraq. Just four days later, while his wife was giving birth, one of their quintuplets died.

By the time Horton returned to Oswego, Illinois, however, things had begun to look brighter: He found that his family had a brand-new $400,000, six-bedroom home, courtesy of a local builder. Other nearby businesses had donated appliances and furnishings, and a local car dealer had donated a $35,000 van to the family.

"I don't think 'thank you' covers it," said Horton, "but that's what comes to mind."

All of us have the ability to brighten the world of those around us. What can you do for your neighbor?

The righteous are generous. (Psalm 37:21)

Lord, help me recognize opportunities to assist those around me.

Remember...and Build Peace

On February 23, 1945, the same day as the famous flag-raising on Iwo Jima, another action took place in the Pacific.

During World War II, over 2,100 people including nuns, and clergy of various denominations were held at Los Banos internment camp in the Philippines. The difficult conditions deteriorated to the point where Gen. Douglas MacArthur got word that the camp was "scheduled for massacre."

Paratroopers of the 11th Airborne were sent to free the prisoners while Filipino guerrillas and U.S. ground forces surrounded the camp. Jesuit Father George Willmann, one of those rescued that day, later wrote that the GIs had "such kindness and sympathy that we could hardly believe these were tough, courageous troops in the midst of an operation that one veteran told me he considered the most hazardous of his career."

The brutality of war cannot be emphasized enough. Honor those who put themselves in harm's way by building peace for all.

Blessed are the peacemakers, for they will be called children of God. (Matthew 5:9)

Prince of Peace, give me the courage to live peace.

Parents–and Kid–in Time Out

Although Elliott's new business, a small coffeehouse featuring musical performances and art receptions, had met with great community acceptance, he, his wife Monica and six-year-old daughter Hannah found themselves busy all the time.

Family time in the coffeehouse's first year meant the family business and nothing else.

One Sunday, after a series of activity packed weekends, plus weekdays of school for Hannah and a full-time office job for Monica, the threesome found themselves on empty.

After Mass, Monica declared a family "time out." She posted the equivalent of a "gone fishing" sign in the window of the coffeehouse, switched off the house telephone ringer, and the three spent the day at home–talking, eating macaroni and cheese, and watching video movies.

At the end of this true day of rest, all three felt renewed and reconnected with what really mattered–each other.

Perhaps today's the day for your "time out"?

**The Sabbath was made for humankind.
(Mark 2:27)**

Father, You want only good things for us. Help me clear the clutter this day to find You.

What the World Needs Now...

While the new millennium has brought exciting advances in technology, medicine and modern conveniences, it has also brought a continuation of the heightened level of insecurity and violence in the world. What is the source of the world's unrest?

According to writer Monica Byrne, what the world needs now is a greater sense of mutual respect, mainly in the form of new and evolved ways of reconciliation. As she writes, "With upheaval, war and death in so many areas of our world, we must look to more powerful means of reconciliation than revenge and brutal retaliation."

Seen another way, perhaps it's as simple as each of us working to become more selfless than selfish.

The next time you face a conflict, practice the simple commandment that Jesus taught: Love others as you love yourself.

Speak the truth...render...judgments that are true and make for peace, do not devise evil...against one another, and love no false oath. (Zechariah 8:16-17)

May Your Spirit, Jesus, walk with us as we work to end violence.

What We Leave Behind

"A Life Barely Noticed, Till It Was Thrown Out" was the title of a *New York Times* article about one Sophie Kaiser, a 94-year-old Brooklynite who had died. Written by Steffie Nelson, it described how the belongings of the woman, who had no family, were thrown into a garbage dumpster by her landlord.

Neighbor's gathered and started to pick through the furniture, china, jewelry and clothes claiming them for their own. "But it was the emergence of a crumpled wedding gown and veil that made everyone pause," wrote Nelson. "The piles of loot suddenly took on the weight of a person's life, one that surely was never intended for the trash."

Kaiser had never married and no one knew why she had owned a wedding dress. There were no answers in the dumpster.

It's easy to ignore people or take them for granted. While we have the chance, let's cultivate compassion for those around us.

**Clothe yourselves with compassion.
(Colossians 3:12)**

Open my eyes to see Your beautiful face in all whom I meet, Dearest Jesus.

What Will You Remember?

George E. Waters, who turned 100 in November, 2004, remembers working in the old Waldorf-Astoria Hotel which was torn down in the 1920s and later relocated to Park Avenue.

Waters was night bell captain for only a few years during the Roaring Twenties but the experience made a big impression on him. Perhaps it was because he was a young man from out of town and New York was exciting. Or, maybe it was encountering celebrities and noted personalities.

Whatever the reason, "This is the only job he ever talks about," says one of his daughters, Barbara Schnaible.

Have you ever wondered what you, or others, will remember about your life should you reach the milestone age of 100?

Now is the time to create fond memories.

In the memory of virtue is immortality.
(Wisdom of Solomon 4:1)

May our lives and actions create pleasant memories, Lord of Life.

God's Scriptwriter

As a child, Barbara Hall says she was "obsessed with Joan of Arc. She was the girl icon that I identified with."

When her own daughter came of age, she began to wonder what it would look like if God tried to get the attention of a teen today. "Then I sort of pictured what my daughter would do if God ever talked to her," Hall explains.

The result was the award-winning and critically-acclaimed television series, *Joan of Arcadia*.

For this series' executive producer-writer, the most controversial idea in the show was that God is available to everybody all the time. "This may not be everyone's idea of God," Hall said. "But I want to celebrate this idea in the show because I believe it to be true."

Every day, each of us does meet God—in a person in need or in a loved one's hug; in bird's song or in sunrise or sunset.

How do you respond to such encounters?

My heart says, "Seek His face!" Your face, Lord, do I seek. Do not hide Your face from me." (Psalm 27:8-9)

Help me to welcome You in Your people, Holy God.

Are the Stars Out Tonight?

If you ever looked at the sky and been amazed by what looks like a barrage of shooting stars, you've probably witnessed a meteor shower.

Most of these meteors are about the size of grains of sand and they appear at certain times of the year. The Leonids, which arrive on or about November 17, are named for the constellation Leo from which their trails appear to originate.

The Leonids were first recognized in 902 A.D. when Chinese and Egyptian astronomers noted that "stars fell like rain." Scientists have since learned that such meteor showers are associated with the breakup of comets. In 1866, Ernst Tempel working in France and Horace Tuttle in the United States both observed a dim comet as the source of the Leonids, now named Comet Tempel-Tuttle.

The universe is full of wonders, whether close at hand, or in the distant sky. Rejoice in them. And thank God.

The glory of the stars is the beauty of heaven, a glittering array in the heights of the Lord. On the orders of the Holy One they stand in their appointed places; they never relax their watches. (Sirach 43:9-10)

Maker of all that is, was or will be, thank You for my place in Your universe.

No Barrier to Achievement

Some think of epilepsy, a common neurological disorder, as a debilitating disease that stops one's life in its tracks. Yet, history tells us that some epilepsy sufferers not only live normal lives, but accomplish wonderful things.

Alfred Nobel, the Swedish chemist who invented dynamite and financed the Nobel Prize had epilepsy.

Poet Alfred Lord Tennyson and mathematician, writer and Anglican deacon Lewis Carroll (Charles Lutwidge Dodgson) also had epilepsy; while the novelist Fyodor Dostoyevsky wove his epileptic experiences into the character of Prince Myshkin in *The Idiot*.

Even Alexander the Great had what was then called "the sacred disease," because it was believed that those with epilepsy were touched by the gods.

These individuals didn't allow the challenge of epilepsy to be a barrier to achievement.

How do you react to challenges, difficulties and trials?

God, the Lord, is my strength; He makes my feet like the feet of a deer, and makes me tread upon the heights. (Habakkuk 3:19)

Blessed Lord, help me see beyond the obstacle in front of me to victory through faith in You.

How to Have a Happy Holiday

If you live in Moline, Illinois, you never have to worry about being alone at Thanksgiving. Folks there know that if they head for a local mall's food court, they will be welcomed to a free dinner by Bob Vogelbaugh, nicknamed "Mr. Thanksgiving."

The celebration started more than thirty years ago when Vogelbaugh, who owns a grocery store, realized that some of his customers had nowhere to go for Thanksgiving. So he invited seven guests to join him for a potluck dinner. The event kept growing. In 2003, more than two thousand people came to dinner.

With the support of donors and hundreds of volunteers, Vogelbaugh serves turkey, stuffing, salad and more. "As for dessert...people show up with a half-dozen pumpkin pies, stacks of angel food cakes," says the host. "We always have enough for everyone."

Think about ways you can extend your hospitality to others. You might start a tradition of your own.

Give thanks in all circumstances.
(1 Thessalonians 5:18)

Generous God, thank You for Your overwhelming blessings. Inspire me to share Your bounty with others.

Decisions...Decisions

Everyday, we make decisions that affect the future in ways we cannot anticipate. It's up to us to reason and act to the best of our ability for one simple reason: that is why God put us here.

English historian and philosopher, Arnold Toynbee, had this to say about the choices we make: "Everyone now alive has been charged with a sacred trust. ...The making of these choices is a heavy burden for us human beings; at the same time, our power to choose and to decide is an open door for hope. This God-given power is our distinctive human characteristic. We are not in the hopeless position of ants or bees, whose actions are dictated by built-in instincts. At the price of being responsible, human beings are free. We are free to choose life and good or to choose death and evil."

In small matters or great ones, always "choose life and good."

Choose life so that you and your descendants may live, loving the Lord your God, obeying Him, and holding fast to Him. (Deuteronomy 30:19-20)

Help me to use my mind and my freedom to choose what is good, holy and life-giving, Blessed Trinity.

Tote Bags Sown in Love

"Women cry when they get (the tote bags)," says Rita Noland who coordinates services for victims of domestic violence. "They're so touched that someone who didn't even know them would care enough to do this."

Noland is referring to the tote bags, sewn by The Sewing Angels of St. Margaret of Scotland Church in Maggie Valley, South Carolina, which are given to the women to use for their personal belongings. "When a woman comes to the shelter, she usually…has nothing," says parishioner Clare Danielewski. She might get "a pillowslip or trash bag to keep her belongings in."

Noland meets victims of domestic violence while they are at a low point in their lives. "They've been called names, hit, sexually abused. They don't feel they deserve anything."

But the tote bags aren't just attractive alternatives to trash bags, they are poignant reminders of the power of love–and of the innate worth of every person.

When you walk through fire you shall not be burned, and the flame shall not consume you. For I am the Lord…You are precious in My sight, and honored, and I love you. (Isaiah 43:2-3,4)

May life-long tender respect characterize marriages, Jesus.

A Legacy of a Different Sort

When an elderly man living in a small apartment in western Spain responded to a newspaper ad promising valuations of art, he wasn't expecting much. The family heirloom that he had evaluated, however, turned out to be "The Baptism of Christ," a lost work by the master El Greco.

Not only that, but the small altarpiece, which had been in the man's family since the mid-19th Century, was dated to a brief span in El Greco's career, when the artist lived in Venice and was developing what would become his unique style. Few pieces of El Greco's work from this period still remain.

Not every mostly-ignored family heirloom will turn out to be worth $1,000,000. But money isn't the only source of value. What in your life might be worth a closer look?

Godliness is valuable in every way.
(1 Timothy 4:8)

Help me to see the true worth of all around me, Spirit of Understanding.

Giving Thanks at All Times

At Thanksgiving, it's natural to contemplate both the many things for which we are grateful, and the importance of gratitude.

In his book, *Gratefulness: The Heart of Prayer*, Benedictine monk David Steindle-Rast, writes, "To be awake, aware and alert are the beginning, middle and end of gratitude. ... Gratefulness is not the result of happiness, it is the cause of happiness."

Here are more thoughts:

"Let us be grateful to people who make us happy; they are the charming gardeners who make our souls blossom."–Marcel Proust

"Reflect upon your present blessings–of which everyone has many– not on your past misfortunes, of which all people have some."–Charles Dickens

"I am beginning to learn that it is the sweet simple things of life which are the real ones after all."–Laura Ingalls Wilder

Cultivate a grateful heart.

With gratitude in your hearts sing psalms, hymns, and spiritual songs to God. (Colossians 3:16)

Beloved Lord, thank You for all You give us. Thank You for all You are–all love, all loveliness, all holiness and all goodness.

An Enriching Revelation

A successful entrepreneur, Robert Young had little contact with or interest in poor people.

That changed when he met septuagenarian Lakota elder Katherine Red Feather. She was his correspondent through the New Mexico-based Adopt a Grandmother Program.

"Here was this woman, this grandmother, living without insulation, plumbing, heating or electricity," on the Pine Ridge Reservation says Young. "There's very little that can prepare you for the poverty one encounters on Pine Ridge."

The Seattle businessman was so moved that he left his corporate life to help build housing for Native Americans. "Before meeting Red Feather, my idea of charity was throwing loose change in a plastic box at a checkout counter," he admits.

Poverty, which may seem distant and insurmountable, exists in our own neighborhoods, cities and states. Seek to help the poor beyond giving loose change. Your own life may change.

Whoever is kind to the poor...will be repaid in full. (Proverbs 19:17)

Merciful Redeemer, make me compassionate toward all who are poor.

Fighting for Women in Iraq

As the Iraq war continues, Yanar Mohamed struggles against domestic violence. She has opened shelters for battered women in Baghdad and Kirkuk—a radical act under a legal system that largely ignores violence against women.

Coming to the shelters without papers or passports, these women even leave their names behind them. They are blamed for the abuse they suffer, accused of bringing dishonor on their families. Because of rigid tradition, some would even be killed if their relatives found them.

The decision to open these shelters grew out of Mohamed's family history: her then teen-aged grandmother had been forced to marry a man 40 years her senior. "I don't want to take us back to the time of my grandmother," said the Iraqi-Canadian architect, and now advocate. "It depends on us—whether we resist or not."

What attitudes or actions toward women, children, the aged, the poor, the handicapped and immigrants need to be resisted?

You shall not wrong or oppress a resident alien, for you were aliens in the land of Egypt. You shall not abuse any widow or orphan. (Exodus 22:21-22)

Just Judge, give me strength to do good.

Having Your Cake and Eating It, Too

According to various polls, the average American gains seven pounds from Thanksgiving to Christmas, and nearly 40 percent of us make losing weight our New Year's resolution. Yet, as we know, many diet programs simply don't work.

In our land of plenty it is difficult to turn down oversized portions. But perhaps that's where the problem lies. Studies show that in nations like France, while people tend to enjoy rich, highly caloric foods daily, they eat smaller portions. The result is less weight gain. Here are tips for healthier eating:

Chew food slowly, savoring every bite.

Choose moderately sized portions.

Eat three meals a day, no more.

Avoid "all you can eat" establishments.

Eat only when you are hungry.

Snack on fruits, veggies and other healthy choices.

On this mountain the Lord...will make for all peoples a feast...of rich food filled with marrow, of well-aged wines strained clear. (Isaiah 25:6)

Lord God, give me the strength to exercise moderation in all areas of my life.

A Breath of Fresh Air

Did you know that each breath you take is composed more of nitrogen than of oxygen?

Every cubic yard of the air around you is, in fact, about 80 percent N2 gas, or nitrogen. While this overabundance of nitrogen, a key component of human proteins, might seem like a wonderful thing, it is virtually useless. Thanks to a handful of bacterial species that can metabolize N2, nitrogen is brought into the overall food chain. Otherwise, it would simply "hang" out in the universe, unused, since no animal, plant or fungus is able to convert the abundant gas into a biologically useful one.

Facts like these reveal how intricate, complex and awe-inspiring God's creation really is. And that includes each and every one of us!

The heavens are telling the glory of God; and the firmament proclaims His handiwork. (Psalm 19:1)

Father Creator, thank You for the blessings You have bestowed upon us. Your creation's wonders are limitless!

One Goat At a Time

The Sisters of Mercy from Pennsylvania are making a difference in the lives of impoverished women in Peru, one goat at a time.

The nuns began a successful livestock-breeding program in Chulucanas, Peru, which helps participants learn marketable skills to help their families. In the process the women's self-esteem and sense of dignity are enhanced.

At the start of the year, women take out small loans to buy two animals; either sheep or goats because they're economical to raise and not prone to disease. At the end of the year, they must give back two animals so the project can continue elsewhere. Participants also take various classes.

"They are beginning to be proud of themselves and are involved in catechetics, health education and ministry," said one of the sisters. "These projects provide minor economic gains that take time. But there have been small but very significant changes."

What small but significant changes can you make?

The patient...are better than the proud in spirit. (Ecclesiastes 7:8)

Redeemer, inspire those who minister to the impoverished.

Guidance through Practical Counsel

During her 12 years as a high school guidance counselor Margaret Boyajian took her responsibilities seriously.

As part of her overall effort to guide students toward college and a fulfilling career Boyajian implemented a system that allowed students to discover, explore and meet their weekly and monthly academic and activities goals.

"There are so many options open to high school students today," says Boyajian. "We try to help them get to know themselves and what kind of career might suit them."

When Boyajian began, roughly 60 percent of the school's students went on to two- or four-year colleges. By the time she retired that number had jumped to 84 percent.

Your work does affect others' lives. Turn your daily toil into a positive, edifying effort.

You are the salt of the earth. (Matthew 5:13)

Holy Spirit, help me recognize even the smallest opportunities to do good, since they often make the greatest difference in others' lives.

About Heaven and Hell

Thought much lately about eternity? About heaven and hell? Even people of faith often hesitate to dwell on the subject, perhaps because it reminds them of their mortality.

Yet, contemplating our lives in light of eternity can help put ourselves in perspective. Gian Carlo Menotti, the renowned composer, had this regret-filled, if thought-provoking idea: "Hell begins on the day when God grants us a clear vision of all that we might have achieved, of all the gifts which we have wasted, of all that we might have done which we did not do. ...To me, the conception of hell lies in two words: *too late!*"

Every single day offers opportunities for us to make earth a little more like heaven, if we would only trust God, avoid regrets and guilt and seek His will.

Then we'll never fear the words, *too late*.

Do not fear death's decree for you...This is the Lord's decree for all flesh. (Sirach 41:3,4)

Beloved and Almighty God help me do my best, to rid myself of regrets and guilt while trusting in Your mercy.

In Search of Justice

"Life is fragile – handle with prayer."

That saying was a favorite of Mamie Till Mobley who died peacefully in 2003. Her only child Emmett Till died in 1955 and there was nothing peaceful about it. He was murdered by racists in Mississippi because, as a visitor from the North, he could not understand that the punishment for a 14-year-old black youngster who whistled at a white woman could be kidnap, torture and death.

Mother Mobley, as she was known, decided that "everybody needed to know what happened to Emmett Till" and insisted on an open casket so that people could see his mutilated body. She later said that "Emmett's death was the impetus for the Civil Rights movement in America."

Mother Mobley became a teacher. She believed, "We must teach our children to weather the hurricanes of life, pick up the pieces and rebuild."

Build up, never tear down.

All who hate a brother or sister are murderers, and...murderers do not have eternal life abiding in them. We know love by this, that He laid down His life for us. (1 John 3:15-16)

Spirit of Courage, direct our path in peace and justice.

Unexpected Millionaire

When Genesio Morlacci retired, the former owner of a dry cleaning shop became a janitor at the University of Great Falls in Montana. So, at his death in 2004 at age 102, no one expected the windfall he left behind. Morlacci left his entire estate–worth $2.3 million–to the university.

How had Morlacci saved that much? He lived a lifetime of hard work, smart investments and old-fashioned thrift–after wearing out shirt collars, for example, he was known to remove them and sew them back on with the frayed side down.

Morlacci's lifetime efforts will now reap benefits long after his death–the University of Great Falls anticipates that his endowment will generate approximately $100,000 a year for scholarships. Not bad for a man many would have dismissed as a simple janitor.

We all have worth beyond the obvious. What's yours, and how can you show it to the world?

You are of more value than many sparrows. (Matthew 10:31)

Lord, help me to do all I can to improve the world.

Advent: Anticipating Christmas

When people talk about "the holidays" what they usually mean is Christmas. We tend to give Advent short shrift.

That's too bad, because Advent can give us the right perspective on December 25. First of all, the word for this season is from the Latin *adventus* meaning coming. It invites us to recognize all comings of Jesus–past, present and future.

The Son of God was born in Bethlehem over 2000 years ago. Through grace, He comes within the hearts of His people day by day. And, finally, as the Christ, Jesus will return in triumph at the Second Coming. Through Advent we realize that Christmas is not merely a commemoration of history, but a celebration of salvation.

Use Advent's four weeks as a time of prayer and spiritual renewal. Wonder at God's everlasting love and His overwhelming gift to each and every one of us: His beloved Child.

God so loved the world that He gave His only Son, so that everyone who believes in Him may not perish but may have eternal life. (John 3:16)

Son of God, Baby of Bethlehem, help us to grow in wisdom and grace as You did–and always, in love.

Pole Climbing Perils

How hard can it be to climb a pole? If it's a telephone pole, it's more difficult than you might think.

Each year, thousands of telephone repair people across the United States attend pole climbing schools to brush up on their technique and safety skills.

There's much to learn: how to spot poles weakened by termites or humidity, which may crack under a climber's weight; what to do if attacked by snakes or bees nesting in the poles; how to avoid being electrocuted; the use of gaffes, the sharp metal pins attached to their boots, for climbing; physical preparedness—weak or weary climbers can lose their grip and slide down in what is know as "pole burning."

These hazards are probably not what you thought of when watching a repair person shimmy up a telephone pole. That's like life. Since things aren't always what they appear to be, be prepared and keep an open mind.

Those who abide in Me and I in them bear much fruit, because apart from Me you can do nothing. (John 15:5)

Lord God, help me be prepared for all life throws at me.

Afghani Artifacts

More than twenty-five years ago, fearing what would happen under the Soviet occupation, the curators of the Kabul Museum in Afghanistan and several government employees wrapped up more than 2,500 priceless artifacts and sealed them in 120 boxes. They vowed to not open the boxes until they were all gathered together again, and it was safe to do so.

The boxes were secretly hidden throughout the country, and survived the Soviets, warlord rule, the Taliban and the American invasion. Some feared that they were lost forever, but when the boxes were gathered and reopened in 2004, all but 100 of the artifacts were accounted for. The museum, meanwhile, had in the intervening years been shelled, looted and burned. Over 5,000 years of history that might have been lost had been saved.

Our past is part of what makes us who we are. What can you do to preserve part of that tradition?

Let us now sing the praises of...our ancestors. (Sirach 44:1)

Help me to remember and honor the past, Eternal Father.

Santa Keeps Giving Back

Santa lives in Kansas City.

At least, people there think so because for more than twenty years, an anonymous man has passed out thousands of dollars in $100 bills in an effort to "give folks some holiday magic to believe in."

The *Kansas City Star* learned that an act of kindness had changed the secret Santa's life in 1971. He was an out-of-work salesman living in his car in Mississippi when the owner of a diner gave him $20 for food and a tank of gas.

Within a few years, his career took off and he started his unusual gift-giving. He also visited the diner-owner whose wife had health problems. "At the time, his $20 seemed like $10,000 to me," says the secret Santa. "So that's exactly how much I paid him back."

Let your own generous spirit make some "holiday magic" through kind deeds.

It is well with those who deal generously and lend, who conduct their affairs with justice. (Psalm 112:5)

Creator of All, thank You for the blessings of my life. Show me how to share Your loving goodness with others.

You're Not Alone

When people are diagnosed with a serious illness they are frightened and feel incredibly alone. Various groups try to help.

Cancer Care, for example, aims to ease the distress of people with cancer. "Our mission is to provide, at no cost, emotional support, information, and practical help to cancer patients and their loved ones," according to executive director Diane Blum.

Cancer Care provides a variety of counseling and informational services to patients, families, caregivers and medical personnel. One of their most popular services is their teleconference series. Specialists discuss a range of subjects that concern people who are living with cancer including state-of-the-art information.

Among Cancer Care's other projects are counseling, in person or on the phone; national support groups; special needs programs for children, African Americans, older adults; and bereavement groups.

Reach out if you need help and hope.

Hope for good things, for lasting joy and mercy. (Sirach 2:9)

Abba, encourage the sick and discouraged to seek the support and help they need.

Mary of Nazareth

Mary of Nazareth was Joseph's wife and Jesus' mother. And while we have little information about her and her life in Roman-occupied Palestine, we do know that Mary is a model of a faith-filled life. Here are just three examples from the Scriptures.

Mary was perplexed at the angel's greeting. She thought through what the angel had said before she said "yes." Mary makes our own questioning and doubting acceptable.

The angel told Mary "do not be afraid." Over the years, she must have struggled with that advice at times, but she lived trusting God always.

Mary dedicated her son to God. She and Joseph brought Jesus to the temple in Jerusalem to present Him. She trusted God as a faithful daughter of Abraham and Sarah.

Look to the example of Mary of Nazareth, mother and disciple of Jesus to inspire your own discipleship.

I believe; help my unbelief! (Mark 9:24)

Jesus, strengthen my faith in You, the Father and the Spirit.

Not-So-Traditional Christmas Traditions

Some Christmas traditions are fairly common: trimming a tree with ornaments, baking, or exchanging gifts. There are some, however, whose Christmas traditions are untraditional.

Pat Schley's family collects nativity scenes from around the world. "I am amazed at how the story of Jesus' birth translates into every culture," she admits.

Cheryl Lagler says that every December, she and her children write the names of friends and family on red and green strips of paper that they make into a chain. "At bedtime throughout the month, we tear a link off and pray for the person written on that strip of paper." Lagler says it is a fun way to "countdown" to Christmas Day and a reminder to pray for loved ones.

What creative ways do you enjoy celebrating holidays? How have those traditions added to the spiritual dimension of your life?

The time came for (Mary) to deliver her child. And she gave birth to her firstborn Son and wrapped Him in bands of cloth, and laid Him in a manger because there was no place for them in the inn. (Luke 2:6-7)

Infant Jesus, help me live a life of tolerance and acceptance of other cultures.

Whispered Prayers

When the Cambodian Dictator Pol Pot came to power in 1975, all religion was decreed abolished. No one would be allowed to go to temple or church, or even to pray. But a boy named Vythy Mimetto found a way.

Each night at the children's camp where he lived, he would quietly say the Our Father and Hail Mary before he went to sleep. "I used to whisper the prayers and keep my hand over my mouth so no one would see," he recalled. "I thought that if I didn't say the prayers every day I would forget them and that there would never be anyone to teach me them again."

Thanks to his faith and that of countless others, Mimetto's worst fear never came true. In fact, since 1990, when Cambodian Christians were once again allowed to worship publicly, the faith there has grown, even flourished.

Even whispered prayer is heard–and answered.

**After I...came as a captive to Nineveh...I was mindful of God with all my heart.
(Tobit 1:10,11)**

Father, may all come to know of Your goodness and mercy.

A Love Lunch

Several weeks before Christmas, Ann was shopping with her five-year-old daughter Elizabeth. Looking at the energy-filled, Christmas-focused child, she thought of her former teacher Marie. Marie's niece, an adorable four-year-old named Angela, had recently lost a long battle with cancer. This would be the family's first Christmas without Angela.

"How about we visit Aunt Marie?" Ann asked her daughter. Elizabeth had called the older woman by that title ever since she could talk.

"I can show her my new book," Elizabeth answered.

Two days later, the three had lunch at a neighborhood diner. Ann listened to Marie and Elizabeth talk. Marie inquired about her grilled cheese sandwich, Elizabeth's favorite. "Is it good?" Marie asked, referring to the sandwich.

"Oh yes, it was," Ann thought.

Although no one can replace a lost loved one, others can fill our broken hearts with their love.

The Father of mercies...consoles us...so that we may be able to console those who are in any affliction. (2 Corinthians 1:3,4)

Gracious God, wrap Your consolation around those who ache with loss and loneliness.

Kids Hope

Virgil Gulker founded Kids Hope USA in the early 1990s. The mentors at the non-profit are chosen from neighborhood churches. Their goal: guiding at-risk youngsters one-on-one through troubling times.

For example, in first grade, Luke was hurt and angry because his father had abandoned the family and his mother was too ill to take proper care of him. But by fifth grade he was named most improved student.

What had changed? Luke's grandfather believes it was a fireman named Mark. As a mentor, he offered the boy what all children need: a long-term, committed relationship with a caring adult.

"They can't comprehend at first that they are important enough that someone who is not getting paid would care exclusively for them," says Virgil Gulker. But they are "important enough" and such special attention works wonders.

How can you help a child know his or her worth and dignity?

(Jesus) said, "Whoever becomes humble like this child is the greatest in the kingdom of heaven. Whoever welcomes one such child in My name welcomes Me." (Matthew 18:2,4-5)

Gentle Jesus, remind us that childlikeness is required of Your disciples.

Creating Beauty

"I decided I wanted to make the city beautiful," said Jim Power, "New York's Mosaic Man" and recipient of an award for his unique talents:

Power decorates lampposts with bits of glass, tile and ceramic, creating glittering designs of public art. His colorful handiwork has caught the attention of academics in the field of folklore and folklife.

Born in Ireland, Power has traveled a "peripatetic path" in life according to one newspaper story. During his military service in Vietnam he first saw mosaics in Buddhist temples. After the Army he was a guitarist, a stonemason and a utility company worker.

"All I really want is for my mosaics to be appreciated, and to have the time and material to finish them," said Power, who lives simply, often supported by the kindness of friends and neighbors. In return, his gift is the creation of something beautiful.

What beauty are you creating?

The Lord (said)...I have filled him with divine spirit, with ability, intelligence, and knowledge in every kind of craft to devise artistic designs. (Exodus 31:1,3-4)

Thank You for the work of artists, Lord.

Working at Friendship

Everyone warned 50-year-old Diane Hendrickson about Eldora, her 81-year-old co-worker in the copy room of a local school. Eldora was a cantankerous old woman whom no one liked.

"If we had to work side-by-side in a hot, peanut-sized room for four hours a day, we had to get along!" Hendrickson vowed.

Off to a rocky start, Hendrickson eventually found a way to win over Eldora. "If I made a point of praising Eldora for her help and neat work (it really was!), her demeanor softened," she explained. "She began to share her life's trials, and I grew to understand her gruff personality. Before long, we'd become a mutual admiration society of two."

People in the school noticed, commenting on Eldora's increased happiness. Hendrickson smiled, answering: "God knew she needed a friend—and I needed her wise counsel for my problems."

Even the most challenging relationship can lead to moments of grace and joy.

Rise before the aged. (Leviticus 19:32)

In each person I meet today, help me to see You, Beautiful Savior.

Thomas Edison and Creative Thinking

"Think outside the box." You have probably heard that phrase in describing how to encourage innovation. But what about thinking inside the bulb?

According to David Armstrong in *Managing by Storying Around*, Thomas Edison had an unusual method for hiring engineers. He gave an applicant a light bulb and asked how much water it held. Some job seekers would use gauges to determine the measurements of the bulb and then calculate the correct answer.

But others would simply fill the bulb with water and pour the water into a measuring cup. The first method took about 20 minutes, the second, about one. Edison only hired engineers in the second group.

Sometimes, we over-complicate our way of looking at things. Before you embark on elaborate plans, ask your self if the simplest, most straightforward way might not be best.

The unfolding of Your words gives light; it imparts understanding to the simple. (Psalm 119:130)

Open my mind to Your counsel, Blessed Trinity, and guide my mind as well as my heart.

Hospitality Knows No Boundaries

"Southern hospitality," refers to Southerners' reputation for charm, grace and willingness to open their homes to others. Genuine hospitality exists elsewhere, too.

When writer Lauren Winner was 16 and a newcomer to New York City, she found boundless hospitality from the Orthodox Jewish community. She was embraced by several families who "knew little about me other than that I was new, my family was far away and I needed somewhere to eat on the Sabbath," she remembers.

Today, as a Virginian, she makes it a point to be hospitable. She says, "We aren't meant simply to invite people into our homes, but into our lives."

Recall those times when you felt out of place, lonely and fearful; when you were a newcomer to a job, a neighborhood or house of worship. Welcome the newcomer. An extended hand or a kind invitation makes a huge difference.

Whoever welcomes one such child in My name welcomes Me. (Matthew 18:5)

God, I pray for the mindfulness to reach out to the lonely and the displaced.

Into the Light

Many homes these days, as well as churches, are taking up the custom of the Advent wreath. More than a ring of evergreens with three purple candles and one pink candle, it's a symbol of light shining in the darkness and of a season that gets too little attention.

Once Thanksgiving is over, Christmas is on everyone's mind. This would be fine if we were talking about the celebration of the birth of Jesus, but, for many, Christmas is more a holiday than a holy day. That's why Advent is so important.

Advent can open our eyes to Christmas, not only as a happy and holy day, but also as the confluence of faith, hope and love in time and eternity. Advent keeps us focused on the coming of the Messiah, the Son of God and our own coming as well—out of the darkness and into the light.

By the tender mercy of our God, the dawn from on high will break upon us, to give light to those who sit in darkness...to guide our feet into the way of peace. (Luke 1:78-79)

Come into our hearts, Emmanuel, You who have saved us from sin and death.

Masons on a Mission

"It never occurred to me that I could do something for the greater good of the world by doing what I love," said Pat Manley.

Manley, a professional mason who has built brick ovens for American restaurants, responded to an e-mail call for volunteers sent to the Masonry Heaters Association of North America. The request came from Ali Ross and Tom Clarke who were working on a plan to build stoves for the Mayan people of Guatemala.

The much-needed concrete and stone stoves would replace the indoor fires then in use. Over the years, the walls of the Mayans' homes became coated with thick black soot from the creosote and smoke. This lead to chronic eye infections, premature blinding, severe burns and tuberculosis.

The Guatemalan Stove Project/Masons on a Mission has now built 1,000 stoves.

Our world would be a better place if we each shared our talents with others.

To each is given the manifestation of the Spirit for the common good. (1 Corinthians 12:7)

Remind us, Holy Spirit, to use our gifts for the common good.

Building Peace from Scratch

Often, activists who seek peace on an international level garner the most attention. However, there are countless local peace workers who mend and nurture relationships–often from scratch and with no assistance–right in their own communities.

Nobel Peace Prize (1976) winner Mairead Corrigan Maguire was galvanized into action after the tragic executions of her young nephews and nieces in Belfast, Northern Ireland. Together with Betty Williams and Ciaran McKeown, Maguire began the Community of Peace People. This broad ecumenical movement which has grown to nearly half a million strong, campaigns for an end to Northern Ireland's centuries old "Troubles."

From one person's effort can emerge a movement of change for the better–for a neighborhood or a nation.

In the days to come...nation shall not lift up sword against nation, neither shall they learn war any more. (Micah 4:1,3)

Holy God, please help me appreciate the importance of my voice for peace and justice.

Special Delivery

At a season when most teens are preoccupied with gifts and holiday celebrations, one group of students spent much of their Christmas assembling care packages for the needy.

Through their local St. Vincent de Paul Society office, a group of religious-education students from the St. Edith Stein Church in Brockton, Massachusetts, filled traditional holiday meal baskets for needy families. The teens assembled the packages in a local warehouse, then worked to box and load the parcels so those requesting assistance feeding their families for the holidays would receive the food in time for Christmas.

The fruit of their efforts, one basket recipient said was that "they gave me, and my kids, something to be thankful for."

A child has been born for us, a son given to us...and he is named Wonderful Counselor, Mighty God, Everlasting Father, Prince of Peace. (Isaiah 7:14)

Infant Jesus, remind us of the true meaning of Christmas.

Seeing the Earth from the Moon

On December 21, 1968, Apollo 8 was launched from Cape Kennedy, Florida. Over the next six days, the spacecraft would orbit the moon ten times.

This mission was one of several made in preparation of an eventual moon-landing. A number of television transmissions were made, including one on Christmas Eve, when the crew read passages from Genesis. Frank Borman, the mission commander, also shared a prayer:

"Give us, O God, the vision which can see Your love in the world in spite of human failure. Give us the faith to trust Your goodness in spite of our ignorance and weakness. Give us the knowledge that we may continue to pray with understanding hearts. And show us what each one of us can do to set forward the coming of the day of universal peace."

Ask God to help us be people of peace.

What does the Lord your God require of you? Only to fear the Lord...to walk in all His ways, to love Him, to serve the Lord...with all your heart and...soul, and to keep the commandments. (Deuteronomy 10:12-13)

Spirit of Peace, inspire us to share Your blessings with family and friends, with neighbors, with all Your children.

Lighting Candles in Bethlehem

When William Da Costa discovered that the city of Bethlehem would not be lighted for Christmas 2003 because of a shortage of funds, he decided to take action from the other side of the world.

Da Costa's fundraising campaign, "Christmas Lights for Bethlehem, Holy Land," asked people to donate money to light Jesus' birthplace. He enlisted the help of a group of local Carmelite nuns. Together, Da Costa and the Carmelites managed to raise over $1,000, enough to keep Manger Square illuminated for the entire 2003 Christmas season.

Without hesitation, a jubilant Da Costa affirmed, "One man can make a difference. It's better to light one candle than to curse the darkness. I apply that to a lot in my life."

There seems to be a limitless supply of opportunities in this world to make a change for the better. Reach out and grab one!

Be rich in good works. (1 Timothy 6:18)

Inspire people to effect positive change in the world, Holy Trinity.

The Other Wise Man

Over the centuries, many traditions have grown up around the wise men from the East who came to worship the infant Jesus.

In the late 19th century, Henry Van Dyke, a Presbyterian minister, wrote a tale which has now become a Christmas classic. In *The Story of the Other Wise Man,* we meet Artaban who misses the three magi by stopping to help a sick man. Then he continued his search: "Though he found none to worship, he found many to help. He fed the hungry, and clothed the naked, and healed the sick, and comforted the captive; and his years passed."

In Jerusalem, thirty-three years later, Artaban is hit by falling debris from an earthquake. The dying magi hears a voice saying, "Inasmuch as thou hast done it unto one of the least of these My brethren, thou hast done it unto Me."

If we choose the path of love, we will always find our way home.

As you did it to one of the least of these who are members of My family, you did it to Me. (Matthew 25:40)

Child of Bethlehem, let me see You and serve You in others.

A Gift for Katie

When families endure the grief of a loved one's death, holidays can be particularly hard.

Sarah Gill-Northcutt's 18-month-old grand daughter Katie had died from birth defects. At Christmas, when she took out the decorations, the first thing Gill-Northcutt saw was Katie's stocking. "What should I do?" she wondered. If it were not hung on the mantel it would be as though Katie had not been part of their lives. But how could she let it hang there empty?

On Christmas Day, the grieving grandmother made a decision. She filled out a slip of paper with a task for each family member: plant a tree, donate a book to the library, buy school supplies for a poor child, etc. Every good deed was to be done in Katie's memory. Everyone loved the idea and it was the start of a new family tradition.

A grieving heart can still be a giving one.

A man who had died...was his mother's only son, and she was a widow...the Lord...had compassion for her. (Luke 7:12,13)

Child of Bethlehem, touch our wounded hearts and show us how to comfort others in their pain.

Of Christmas Peace

Charles Appleton Wadsworth, a son of poet and scholar Henry Wadsworth Longfellow, was seriously wounded in 1863, the height of the Civil War. During his recovery, his father wrote a poem which has become a familiar carol:

"I heard the bells on Christmas day
Their old familiar carols play
And mild and sweet the words repeat,
Of peace on earth, good will to men. ...
And in despair I bowed my head:
'There is no peace on earth,' I said,
'For hate is strong, and mocks the song
Of peace on earth, good will to men.'
Then pealed the bells more loud and deep:
'God is not dead, nor doth He sleep;
The wrong shall fail, the right prevail,
With peace on earth, good will to men."

Do all you can to build peace each day, all year long.

A harvest of righteousness is sown in peace for those who make peace. (James 3:18)

Christ Jesus, show me how to imitate You as a person of justice, mercy and peace.

Tidal Wave of Aid

The world turned upside down for millions of people whose homes and communities were wiped away by the tsunami that struck south Asia on December 26, 2004.

But if the natural disaster with countless deaths in its wake was horrific, the response by the rest of the world was breathtaking. We expect governments, especially of wealthy nations like the United States, to assist recovery efforts. But it was individual people who saw the overwhelming need and, from the first day, sent supplies and money to relief agencies.

There were the youngsters in a Seattle suburb who stood in the rain selling "Hot Chocolate for Tidal Wave Relief." Then there was the Kentucky woman who turned a New Year's Eve party into a fundraiser; and the Malaysian-born man who gave a day's proceeds from his Brooklyn restaurant to the effort.

Let us continue to use our time and talents to lift His children from misery.

Whoever welcomes one such child in My name welcomes Me, and whoever welcomes Me welcomes not Me but the One who sent Me. (Mark 9:37)

Spirit of Hope, steer my course that I may always do Your gracious will.

The Ultimate Challenge

Suzanna McNamara would tell you that the thrill of exploring the world would pale in comparison to what she faces simply going to work every day in New York City.

That's because Suzanna's job involves a highly personal, important element that mere adventures lack. As a literacy teacher at a Bronx high school, Suzanna teaches English to teenage immigrants from 30 countries in Africa, Latin America, Asia and Eastern Europe. The teens, most of whom are refugees whose education has been upset by wars, family upheaval or economic turmoil, speak more than 22 different languages.

McNamara says that a stint tutoring Spanish-speaking inmates in a New Mexico prison sparked her love of teaching and of helping eliminate "the plight of people who are marginalized by language problems."

Language is the most basic form of human communication. Use it well and encourage others to do the same.

The king commanded his palace master Ashpenaz to bring some of the Israelites...they were to be taught the literature and language of the Chaldeans. (Daniel 1:3,4)

Help me realize how powerful and precious language is, Holy Trinity.

Advice from the Cookie Man

In his official portrait, Wally Amos—considered by many to be the father of the gourmet cookie industry—is shown holding a pitcher in one hand and a glass of lemonade in the other. The reason? Amos has turned lemons into lemonade so often in his life that he thought the image quite fitting.

A perennial optimist, Amos refuses to acknowledge that obstacles are anything other than stepping-stones to success. In a career that has spanned decades, he has made it to the pinnacle of success several times—only to lose everything and be forced to start over. But he's never lost faith.

"You have the trust and faith to let go and not agonize," he says. "Don't waste your time worrying. Analyze the situation and focus on solutions. There is always an answer."

Disappointments and difficulties—even failures—are part of life; it's how we handle them that makes all the difference.

Trust in the Lord, and do good...Take delight in the Lord...Commit your way to the Lord; trust in Him...Be still before the Lord, and wait patiently for Him. (Psalm 37:3,4,5,7)

Help me, Master, to be as optimistic about myself and others as You are.

Crestfallen No More

Dr. M.M.M. Sameem refuses to let hope wash out to sea with the tide.

In the wake of the tsunami that devastated Asia in 2004, Dr. Sameem, the government medical officer for several coastal Sri Lankan towns, is a great force in aiding those in refugee camps.

Dr. Sameem considers the health of the 5,187 people living in a dozen refugee camps in Pottuvil, Sri Lanka, his personal responsibility. The population of the town before the disaster was 38,000.

"So many people are affected by the tsunami," said Sameem. "They don't have money and they are suffering."

Dr. Sameem charges only 100 rupees (roughly $1), for a visit, and will take nothing at all if a patient cannot afford his fee.

No matter what the odds, one person truly can make a difference for all.

Recovery lies in the hands of physicians, for they too pray to the Lord that He grant them success in diagnosis and in healing, for the sake of preserving life. (Sirach 38:13)

In the face of disaster, Loving Father, let Your generosity strengthen us.

Sweet Memories

Although his best-selling books have virtually nothing to do with cuisine, author Mitch Albom loves to talk about food.

When asked how he likes to celebrate New Year's Eve, Albom admits that, in his family, they "eat our way to midnight." They sample delicacies such as Belgian chocolate, chocolate chip ice cream and pecan pie. "Sweets are our weakness," he says.

Although Albom's first best-seller, *Tuesdays with Morrie,* is about the impact a college mentor had on his life, it was his grandmother Ruth, who taught him about cooking and eating. "I learned how food was put together by watching her make things like French toast and fried cutlets," he says. "I got my love of sweets from her...my love of food."

It has been said that food not only nourishes our bodies but also our souls. Savor each and every bite. Food of any kind is a gift in a hungry world.

Delight yourself in rich food. (Isaiah 55:2)

Generous God, remind me that I have a responsibility to feed the hungry in my own community.

Sounds in the Silence

There are probably few people in our hectic, noisy world who have not wished at some time for some blessed silence. But silence is more than the absence of sound, it is a chance to hear God more clearly.

Rev. Frederick William Faber, a 19th century writer of devotional literature and composer of hymns, including "Faith of Our Fathers," had this to say about listening for the Divine voice:

"There is hardly ever a complete silence in our soul. God is whispering to us well nigh incessantly. Whenever the sounds of the world die out in the soul, or sink low, then we hear these whisperings of God.

"God is always whispering to us, only we do not always hear, because of the noise, hurry, and distraction which life causes as it rushes on."

Find the time and place to quietly open your soul to God's whisperings. You never know what you'll hear.

For God alone my soul waits in silence...He alone is my rock and my salvation, my fortress. (Psalm 62:1,2)

Let me listen to You with my whole being, Beloved Lord.

Also Available

Have you enjoyed volume 40 of *Three Minutes a Day*? These other Christopher offerings may interest you:

- **News Notes** – published 10 times a year on a variety of topics of current interest. One copy as published is free; quantity orders are also available.

- **Ecos Cristóforos** – Spanish translations of selected News Notes. Issued six times a year. One copy as published is free; quantity orders are also available.

- **Wall or Desk Appointment Calendar and Monthly Planner** – The Calendar offers an inspirational message for each day. The Monthly Planner, with its trim, practical design, also offers a monthly inspirational message.

- **Videocassettes** – Christopher videos range from wholesome entertainment to serious discussions of family life and current social and spiritual issues.

For more information on The Christophers or to receive **News Notes, Ecos Cristóforos** or a catalogue:

The Christophers
12 East 48th Street
New York, NY 10017
Phone: 212-759-4050 / 888-298-4050
E-mail: mail@christophers.org
Website: www.christophers.org